T3-BOB-463

Reflections on Aging

A Spiritual Guide

Leo E. Missinne, M. Afr.

LIGUORI
PUBLICATIONS

One Liguori Drive
Liguori, Missouri 63057-9999
(314) 464-2500

Imprimi Potest:
William A. Nugent, C.SS.R.
Provincial, St. Louis Province
The Redemptorists

Imprimatur:
Monsignor Maurice F. Byrne
Vice Chancellor, Archdiocese of St. Louis

ISBN 0-89243-319-1
Library of Congress Catalog Card Number: 89-64247

Contents

Acknowledgments

This book is only a beginning....The reader has to complete and finish the story. My sources of information are my conversations with God and ongoing conversations with friends, colleagues, and older people.

I am most grateful to all my students at the University of Nebraska and the University of Southern California. They have been a source of inspiration. Their search for meaning in the different events of their lives has helped me find some possible answers to my own search.

My contacts with so many wise older people opened a door for looking toward older age as a time of wisdom and grace.

The Christian values that I inherited from the example of my parents are the foundation of the ideas expressed in this book. My father and mother created the space where I could grow in God's presence during the different seasons of my life. To them I dedicate this book with love and affection.

I am also grateful to B.J. Hateley, Jan Matan, and Jackie Melvin for helping me articulate my ideas.

I owe a special word of thanks to Edna Mae Miller for her generous and skillful assistance in typing and retyping the manuscript. Thanks also to James A. Thorson, Director of the Gerontology Program at the University of Nebraska, and David A. Peterson, Associate Dean of the Andrus Gerontology Center at the University of Southern California, for giving me extra time to write.

My final thanks go to Julie Kelemen, this book's project editor. She took my knowledge and experience in the field of aging and combined it with her perspective as a younger person to produce a balanced view of aging in today's world.

Introduction

In the last 20 years, authors have written many books and articles about aging. Most have tried to analyze older age. They have studied the biological, psychological, and social aspects of aging — how to live longer, what a person has to do in order to have a happy and healthy older age, and whether people agree or disagree with certain stereotypes about older people. Percentages and statistics play a very important role in explaining the reality of being an older person.

These pages, however, will reflect on more fundamental questions of human existence in older age: What is life all about? What is the meaning of suffering? What is the purpose of living as a handicapped older person? How will we understand our death and dying process? Is there a specific spirituality and theology of older age?

A few studies have concentrated on these questions in more recent literature. Thomas R. Cole and Sally A. Gadow in *What Does It Mean to Grow Old? Reflections From the Humanities*[1] studied the fundamental aspects of meaning, death, risk, life review, frailty, strength, and morality in older age. Sharon R. Kaufman in her work *The Ageless Self: Sources of Meaning in Late Life*[2] examined how older people construct and maintain their sense of self in late life through internalized events or principles that become values giving meaning to their lives. In his book *Learn to Grow Old*,[3] Swiss psychiatrist Paul Tournier has also reflected on the meaning of life and suffering in older age.

These authors' different approaches inspire us with their new insights and spiritual foundations. Through careful listening to the stories and reflections of older people, we all can be helped to understand how to experience and face the events of older age. It is a particularly complex quest for meaning. A time will come for each of us (if it isn't here already) when we will be faced with learning to accept what God has prepared for us. It is then that we'll realize that neither friends nor guides can find the meaning of life and suffering for us; we have to discover it for ourselves and follow the lonely way, taking responsibility for our own approaches, understandings, and explanations. We need to accept the pain and the happiness of being ourselves in our search for meaning.

I am a searcher too — a human being in search of some deeper meaning, in search of values which give a sense of purpose to my daily life and to my life in general. After many hesitations and doubts, after trying one way and then another, after meeting friends and enemies, after finding provisional meanings in some success and some defeat, I can still say with Dante, "In the middle of the way of our life, I find myself in a dark wood."[4] This dark wood has had some open spaces where I found sun and happiness when I encountered a human being who went some distance with me during a certain time. Thereafter I again entered the dark forest, knowing that no one could live my life, be happy, or suffer in my place. The only real encounter was an encounter with God, who is giving meaning to my long pilgrimage toward finding truth and meaning.

Some friends left me because they would not go with me into the darkness. They judged me, and with the pain of their judgment, I wandered again into that dark place where each tree can be a grace or an obstacle. Traveling by myself was and still is not only frightening but also a challenging and great experience. Only in the middle of a dark wood can we listen to the voice of God whispering to us the deeper meaning of our lives. Many times I have felt like Elijah seeking God, as it is described in the First Book of Kings:

There he came to a cave, where he took shelter. But the word of the LORD came to him, "Why are you here, Elijah?"...The LORD said, "Go outside and stand on the mountain before the LORD; the LORD will be passing by." A strong and heavy wind was rending the mountains and crushing rocks before the LORD — but the LORD was not in the wind. After the wind there was an earthquake — but the

LORD was not in the earthquake. After the earthquake there was fire — but the LORD was not in the fire. After the fire there was a tiny whispering sound. When he heard this, Elijah hid his face in his cloak and went and stood at the entrance of the cave. A voice said to him, "Elijah, why are you here?"

(1 Kings 19:9, 11-13)

Your Own Quest
for the Meaning of Aging

The feeling of being alone in a dark wood, in touch with God, or searching to find the voice of God can be the beginning of new adventures and answers in your quest for meaning.

Being alone in answering questions about the meaning of *your* life and *your* death does not mean that you did not and do not need other people. We *all* need one another, but nobody can find meaning for the other or respond for the other. Only *you* can respond to the events of your life, give meaning to them, and take responsibility for your own answers. We also need to be in contact with the different stages of our own lives. You must remember the teenager you were 50 years ago in order to understand your search for God and yourself today. We need to meet all kinds of people so that we can find ourselves. Young people need older people just as older people need young people in order to become more themselves and more human. That humanizing process will teach us that there is a child behind the mask of each older face, just as there is already an older person behind the mask of each young face. Your encounter with others and yourself must be fundamentally an encounter in which you *listen* to yourself and others. These encounters with God and with others can be painful, but they always are challenging. People can hurt us, or we can hurt them.

Your encounters with problems, realizations, and misfortunes are always valuable, as long as you learn from them. Our experiences, happy or sad, can inspire young people only if we older people will *communicate* with them. Communication involves both talking *and* listening on the part of both parties. In talking about our experiences, we older people can find an exciting and positive meaning in being older. Young people, as they converse with us, may be inspired in their own search for meaning. We all can learn from grief as well as from pleasure.

To a certain measure we are responsible for our old age, or to be more concrete, for our older face. The "epiphany" of your face will tell others and yourself how you are aging. How you digest different experiences, the good and the bad ones, will have an impact on your eyes, skin, and face. Wrinkles do not lie. The state of your eyes will show how and what you have observed. No one has more beautiful eyes than certain children and certain older people!

Older age is a reality of life just as rain and sun, good days and bad days, birth and death, are realities. Accept older age, for where there is graceful older age, there is awareness of yourself, others, happiness, pain, and life in the face of your finitude. This means that older age will be an important source of dignity but also of burden, not only for you but also for other people who are in contact with you.

We older people are not only able to find meaning in our own lives but may also *give* meaning to the lives of others through our positive examples, or even through our sickness or helplessness. Many nurses, social workers, and others who study aging and the problems of aging people have found meaning in their own lives by taking care of older people or being in contact with them. Meaning is not only an aspect of our individual lives, it also has a social aspect. What we are and what we do influence the people around us. That is one of the reasons why older people are in this world. All kinds of older people — happy and sad ones, healthy and sick ones — remind others of what they are or will be one day.

If there is no meaning in older age for ourselves or others, why not allow older people to kill themselves or allow society to kill them?

In his novel *Welcome to the Monkey House*,[5] Kurt

Vonnegut wrote about a beautiful restaurant where older people between their 65th and 66th birthdays would invite relatives and friends to an expensive and elegant dinner. After dinner the friends and relatives would leave the room through one door and the older person through another, beyond which he or she would meet the death of his or her choice.

If there is no meaning in older age, wouldn't it be better if we could die at a chosen time so that we are not a burden for society and for ourselves? *Is* there meaning in life for an older person, and can old age be meaningful for those around the elderly? These are the fundamental questions that will influence not only our way of life but also our retirement and our own death and dying process.

One of the key problems of aging is the frightening thought that there might not be much meaning to life in old age. Gradually it dawns on people that someday they might not be needed at their places of work, in their families, and in society. When people become aware of the gradual decrease in their physical and mental powers, they begin fearing that they may become useless and unwanted — a burden to others. The people who are most susceptible to this are those who have led a very active life, striven for great achievement, and absorbed their minds in the pursuit of great projects in life. These people will feel a real *terror* at the sudden lack of purpose and meaning in their lives at retirement time.[6]

Is there meaning in older age? Is there meaning in *your*

suffering in older age? Is aging different for a clergy person like me than it is for a layperson?

The best way for me to answer all these difficult questions is to reflect on them and talk about them with some good friends. I also talk about them to myself as I contemplate and pray about my own aging process. One day I'll discover some aspects of that mystery when I have the patience to listen to myself and to others who are struggling too. I will let the Spirit guide me. Nobody can tell me the meaning of life and my sufferings. I have to discover it myself so that it can be a genuine personal answer. It is a very subjective matter. There is no causal relationship, it is not a consequence of a circumstance, and it is not the result of an intellectual discussion. It is a permanent challenge — a building up and a destroying, a changing and a creating — on the foundation of values I am trying to live by.

It is not because we do not discover some meaning at a certain point of time that there is no meaning. T. Earl Yarborough in his article "Push Back the Curtain of Darkness" offers an inspiring example of a little girl that illustrates the unveiled mystery of meaning. The story can be translated into what an older person can do in other circumstances.

My daughter, Laura Lowe, has committed her life to lending a helping hand to little children. She teaches in the Head Start Program in Charlotte,

North Carolina. Recently, she told me the following story about a three-year-old girl in her class. The teachers had just taken the boys and girls out on the playground for their play period. As the children scattered around the grounds, they found a big piece of broken glass. At that moment, a little girl walked up to Laura and said, "I can pick up the glass and it won't hurt me." This child had been born without arms, and she had been fitted with artificial arms that ended with steel clamps. She walked over and picked up the broken glass and put it in the trash can. At that moment all her classmates and teachers burst into applause. The little girl with the steel arms and hands accepted the tribute with a beautiful smile on her face. All of a sudden she had become a heroine because she had been able to do something — to be of real service to others — in a way the others could not. The beautiful attitude of this little girl will take her through life in a positive way. Life for her will be meaningful. She deserved the applause.[7]

No situation is totally without meaning. No human being lacks meaning either, but it is up to each of us to discover it. To be older and/or sick reminds us of what life is all about — that it's a short journey. For a spiritually inclined person, aging's signs of physical (and sometimes mental) regression can be transformed through God's grace to mean that a reunion with God is near. It can be a time of fulfillment in which we can, through a life review, process and complete our unfinished business with God, others, and ourselves.

In the following chapters I will share some ideas about the second half of the human journey. It is not my intention to do this as a teacher or as somebody who "knows it all." I am, in fact, a beggar.

A beggar is a person who has been suffering and is still suffering — looking for something that will satisfy the hunger for meaning and that will give life to personal existence.

I want to share these reflections as your friend — a companion in your search for meaning as you grow closer to God in maturity.

We are all beggars seeking fulfillment because we are all, in one sense or another, needy. To be needy is what being human is all about. Someone who has everything and doesn't need other people is no longer a human being.

So the beggar who has written these reflections will show you fellow beggars where you can find something to eat, something to fulfill your needs, some bread, just plain bread. I will not give you bread, but I will show you where you can find it. And if one day you do find some bread, may you do as an old Asian proverb teaches us: "If you find but two loaves of bread, sell one of the two loaves and with the money, buy yourself some beautiful white flowers to feed your soul."

The beauty of flowers, the beauty of nature, and the beauty of other people will help you become more human and find some meaning in your relations with yourself, other people, and God. Beauty will help you love. This means that all physical, psychosocial, and financial techniques people offer you to help you have a good older age must be accompanied by beauty and love. This is necessary if you want to have an older age full of grace and wisdom.

Aging is one of the most essential human processes, one that can be denied only with great harm. Every man and woman who has discovered or rediscovered his or her own aging has a unique opportunity to enrich the quality of his or her own life and that of every fellow human being.[8]

SOURCES

[1]Thomas R. Cole and Sally A. Gadow, *What Does It Mean to Grow Old: Reflections From the Humanities* (Durham, NC: Duke University Press, 1986).

[2]Sharon R. Kaufman, *The Ageless Self: Sources of Meaning in Late Life* (Madison, WI: University of Wisconsin Press, 1986).

[3]Paul Tournier, *Learn to Grow Old* (New York: Harper and Row, 1983).

[4]Dante Alighieri, "Inferno" canto I, in *The Divine Comedy*.

[5]Kurt Vonnegut, Jr., *Welcome to the Monkey House* (New York: Delacorte Press, 1970).

[6]Alfons S. Deeken, *Growing Old and How to Cope With It* (San Francisco: Ignatius Press, 1986), p. 68.

[7]T. Earl Yarborough, "Push Back the Curtain of Darkness," *Loss, Grief, and Care: A Journal of Professional Practice,* Vol. 1 (Fall 1986, Winter 1986-87), pp. 165-166.

[8]Henri J. Nouwen and Walter J. Gaffney, *Aging: The Fulfillment of Life* (Garden City, NY: Image Books, Doubleday, 1976), p. 154.

CHAPTER ONE

The Meaning of Life in Older Age

Life is lived forward but understood backward.

Sören Kierkegaard

Reflections on the meaning of life in older age are not easy to make or communicate because they deal with two extremely difficult topics — older age and life itself. Life is full of mysteries. Add the specific issue of older age to the search for life's meaning, and you have quite a complicated matter. No science will ever be able to explain and understand the content of what it means to be older because aging is part of life, and life is a mystery not a problem. Human beings make problems. Mysteries are part of God's gift to us.

"Reflecting On" Versus "Explaining" Life

If an extraterrestrial being were to visit Earth, scientists could dissect and analyze it in order to obtain a great deal of information. That information would likely become very important in scientific milieus because we would have explained a part of that extraterrestrial being. However, in order to dissect that being, people would necessarily have to kill it. There would no longer be any opportunity to attempt communication or even friendship with it. True, we would have information about how the creature is put together, but we will have killed that living being. Too much science and too many techniques can kill the most important aspects of life.

That is the reason I prefer to reflect upon, rather than explain, one of the most fundamental issues of older age — finding its meaning or purpose. What is the meaning of life in older age, or *has* older age a meaning? It is a philosophical question that has many implications.

The question of meaning in old age is not merely an academic inquiry; it has implications for the quality of life for real people in today's world. Old age is a period when the shape of life as a whole comes into view. At this point in life we older people may try to see things on a wider scale. Totality may be metaphysically unattainable, but the drive toward totality — the search for meaning — appears at a point when the task of life is about to be completed.

Are you asking yourself these questions?

- Why am I still alive as a frail, sick, or handicapped older person?

- What is the point of my life?
- Why do I have to continue to live when I am no longer accepted in the society in which I am living?

These questions are familiar to aging people or people who are in contact with sick older people and concerned with their well-being. To reflect on these questions and arrive at different possible answers will help people live as human beings until the last days of their lives.

Others Have Wondered About the Same Things

The question of meaning in life has been approached in absolutely contradicting ways. The Buddha said that one must immerse oneself in the river of life and let that question drift away. Jean-Paul Sartre wrote, "All existing things are born for no reason, continue through weakness, and die by accident. It is meaningless that we are born; it is meaningless that we die."[1]

Leo Tolstoy wrote about "life arrest" — a crisis of meaning in life — in his book *My Confession, My Religion: The Gospel in Brief.*

The question, which in my fiftieth year had brought me to the notion of suicide, was the simplest of all questions, lying in the soul of every man from the undeveloped child to wisest sage: "What will come from what I am doing now, and may do tomorrow? What will come from my whole life?" otherwise expressed — "Why should I live? Why should I wish for anything? Why should I do anything?" Again, in other words: "Is there any meaning in my life which will not be destroyed by the inevitable death awaiting me?"[2]

And he wrote further:

Five years ago a strange state of mind began to grow upon me: I had moments of perplexity, of a stoppage, as it were, of life, as if I did not know how I was to live, what I was to do....These stoppages of life always presented themselves to me with the same question: Why? and what for?...These questions demanded an answer with greater and greater persistence and like dots, grouped themselves into one black spot.[3]

Author and philosopher Albert Camus believed that all people are looking for a "why" that they never find, and they are doomed to live in absurdity. He wrote, "I have seen many people die because life for them was not worth living. From this I conclude that the question of life's meaning is the most urgent of all."[4] He illustrates the dilemma of human life in the following way:

Of whom and of what indeed can I say: "I know that!" This heart within me I can feel, and I can judge that it exists. This world I can touch and I, likewise, judge that it exists. There ends all my knowledge, and the rest is construction....This very heart which is mine forever will remain indefinable to me. Between the certainty I have of my existence and the content I try to give to that assurance, the gap will never be filled. Forever I shall be a stranger to myself.[5]

Finding Life's Meaning Is Good for Your Health

Many psychologists agree that a lack of meaning in life, or meaninglessness, is often the origin of neurotic or psychotic behavior. Carl Jung felt that the clinical syndrome of meaninglessness was a very common phenomenon in his practice as a psychiatrist. He wrote, "Absence of meaning in life plays a crucial role in the etiology of neurosis. A neurosis must be understood, ultimately, as a suffering of a soul which has not discovered its meaning....About a third of my patients are not suffering from any clinically definable neurosis but only from the senselessness and aimlessness of their lives."[6]

Viktor Frankl stated that most of his patients who came to see him as a psychiatrist suffered from an existential neurosis, which had meaninglessness at its root. Other twentieth-century psychologists such as Salvatore Maddi, Benjamin Wolman, and Nicholas Hobbs agree that the failure to find meaning in life is often the origin of disorganized or abnormal behavior.

But we do not need to be famous psychologists to see the meaninglessness in the lives of so many people today. Meaninglessness is manifested in the disease of our time — boredom. People find their jobs boring, their marriages boring, their friends boring, their studies boring, and sometimes even their vacations boring! For this reason many people choose to do self-destructive things: They drive as fast as possible, steal, or take drugs in order to have the feeling that they are *living*. Such reckless behavior helps them feel that they have a purpose in life for at least a few hours or days. They are looking for something exciting, and they find it briefly when the police pick them up. They can dress in extravagant clothes or become members of a gang or drink too much…all so they are at least "existing" for some people who observe them.

Each human being needs to find meaning in life. In his book *When All You've Ever Wanted Isn't Enough*,[7] Rabbi Harold Kushner analyzes the questions of meaning in today's culture. Everyone attempts to find meaning, at least at certain moments in life. In fact it is the privilege of a human being to be able to *ask* the question of meaning. Animals never reflect on what they are or the purpose of their actions; they just follow their instincts. The search for meaning confronts every human being, young as well as old. This search can become tragic and urgent when one is in a period of crisis, when one suffers the loss of a relative or friend, or when a person feels that the end of life is near.

Finding the Road to Meaning

We can find some answers to the questions concerning meaning of life in the application of Viktor Frankl's theory. His theory addresses the crises older people often experience in retirement, in the death of a spouse, or in the common limitations and sufferings of older age. These crises can offer many new and fresh invitations to find meaning in the events which can cause us to ask ourselves, "Why do I have to go through these sufferings? I have always been a good person. I always tried to live as a good Christian. Why should I have to go through so much suffering in my older days?"

It is surprising that only once in a while do success or happiness push us to ask ourselves the same questions. In fact many times we don't trust a state of happiness and success because we fear that something so good cannot last too long. This is what the ancient Greeks thought when they said that one can call no man happy until he is dead.

In his book *Man's Search for Meaning,* Frankl

described his life experiences in a concentration camp through the framework of his theory.[8] As a professor of psychiatry and neurology at the University of Vienna, Frankl did not challenge the work of Sigmund Freud, Alfred Adler, and Carl Jung — his psychoanalytical predecessors. Frankl understood the importance of Freud's description of sexual drives and needs. He agreed with certain aspects of Adler's theory concerning the will to power, the will to assert one's self, and Jung's view of human aspirations toward integration. But Frankl firmly believed that what inspires a person most deeply is the will to *meaning* — the innate desire to give one's life as much meaning as possible.

Having Values Is the Key

Frankl contended that a person can find meaning in life by believing in values. The values a person holds will give meaning to and explain personal behavior. Frankl distinguished three different categories of values: creative, experiential, and attitudinal ones.

Creative Values: A person can give meaning to life by believing and realizing creative values — by achieving, by "doing something." Some examples of creative values are writing a book, building a house, organizing a group of volunteers, planning a reunion, painting, studying, or generally doing something which has personal meaning. The point is that a person has to *do* something in order to find meaning in life. For example, in doing something for God, the Church, or some other congregation they belong to, people often find that such tasks give purpose and meaning to their lives. An active life serves the purpose of giving them opportunities to realize values through creative work — through making a new creation.

Experiential Values: Another way to discover meaning in life is to realize your experiential values by experiencing the good, the true, and the beautiful, or by knowing a single human being in all his or her uniqueness. To experience one human being as unique means to love that person. Love, beauty, and truth provide reasons for continuing to live. Love of a husband or wife gives many people the most profound meaning in their lives. Love of grandchildren gives many older people a deep sense of satisfaction which can give much meaning to grandparents' lives. Love for God or the Church can fulfill older people. Living in beautiful homes — cozy places where they can enjoy beauty — is another example of experiential values giving meaning to life that will keep older persons *living*, not merely existing.

Attitudinal Values: A person may, however, be in such great distress that neither creative nor experiential values can provide meaning. Such a person can still find meaning in the way that he or she faces affliction, suffering, or sickness. By accepting personal suffering, people can realize attitudinal values. The possibility of discovering values through suffering exists to the very last moment of life. An honorable suffering is perhaps the highest achievement possible for a human being. No one can better exemplify what life is all about than a person who is sick or dying. Healthy human beings need to be in contact with sick people in order to appreciate their own health or youth. Frankl illustrated this attitudinal-value theory with a story that is filled with wisdom for older people:

A colleague doctor turned to me because he could not come to terms with the loss of his wife who had died two years before. His marriage had been very happy and he was now extremely depressed. I asked him quite simply, "Tell me what would have happened if you had died first and your wife had survived you?"

"That would have been terrible," he said. "How my wife would have suffered!"

"Well, you see," I answered, "your wife has been spared that and it was you who spared her, though of course you must now pay by surviving and mourning her." In that very moment, his mourning had been given a meaning — the meaning of sacrifice.[9]

Although Frankl does not specifically relate his theory about attitudinal values to elderly people's problems, what he has to say is very pertinent to aging persons. An older person, who either chooses not to or is not allowed to work or who can no longer work because of a disability or sickness, may be required to set aside the realization of creative values — trying to accomplish things. However, an aging person still can find deep meaning in beauty and in loving relationships with family and friends. If even these are not possible, there is still the hope for achieving the highest of all values — facing personal sickness or distress with the right attitude. The courageous attitude of a suffering person can inspire people who are, themselves, seeking purpose and meaning in life.

Whenever one is confronted with an unacceptable, unavoidable situation, whenever one has to face a fate that cannot be changed, that is, an incurable disease, such as an inoperable cancer, just then is one given a last chance to actualize the highest value, to fulfill the deepest meaning, the meaning of suffering. For what matters above all is the attitude we take toward suffering, the attitude in which we take our suffering upon ourselves.[10]

The meaning of life is found not in what we expect from life but in what life, circumstances, and events expect from us.

It did not really matter what we expected from life, but rather what life expected from us. We needed to stop asking of ourselves as those who were being questioned by life — daily and hourly. Our answer must consist, not in talk and meditation, but in right action and in right conduct. Life ultimately means taking the responsibility to find the right answer to its problems and to fulfill the tasks which it constantly sets for each individual.[11]

Frankl makes a point that we all, especially the elderly, need to hear. We are all *responsible* for the answers we must give to the questions life will ask us in both younger and older days. If the time and events that have passed have been good, we older people must take the responsibility to continue the good and to make it better. If what has passed has been unjust, we must take the responsibility to change what we can and to commit ourselves to answering life's questions with "right action" and "right conduct." Older age challenges us to act as free human beings addressing all of aging's attending problems in our own unique human ways. Older persons have the opportunity and responsibility of answering this challenge with a response that can be an example to the younger generation and an inspiration to peers.

Human life, under any circumstances, never ceases to have a meaning. This infinite meaning of life includes deprivation, suffering, dying, and death. The comprehension of infinite meaning in one's life is many times preceded by provisional or short-term experiences which also give meaning to life. To help another human being, to create a new organization, to enjoy an evening of beautiful music, will give a person meaning for a certain time and a certain place. But there is no time that is more appropriate for a union of our immediate and ultimate purposes in life than that of older age. The closer we come to looking death in the face, the more each day and each event has a sense of the infinite in it. When we are young, we are frequently too busy discerning momentary, immediate meanings to be drawn to the search for ultimate meaning. In old age, however, when time is more available and work no longer preoccupies our minds and spirits, we are finally free to explore deeper meanings and to rely on past experiences and glimpses of ultimate meaning.

C.S. Lewis, a renowned Cambridge professor of medieval literature, was also an apologist for the Christian faith. He wrote about so-called "glimpses" of ultimate meaning that occur throughout life. He called them "glimpses of joy" and suggested that a sudden awareness of beauty, a momentary sense of deep inner peace, or an experience of undefined longing is really a pointer or marker that directs us to the ultimate meaning in life — to God.[12] What better time than old age to bring all the glimpses together and live each day with a fuller grasp of ultimate meaning.

There are perhaps no persons better prepared to address the question about life's ultimate meaning than older persons whose lives have centered around many provisional meanings. For older persons facing the inescapable reality of death, the time is right to put all the "glimpses" together in an attempt to find the ultimate meaning in life and to find out if their lives have made a difference in the world.

How to Find Values

You can find values through dialogue — nondirective dialogue. In order to discover the meaning of life, it's necessary to *talk* about it with someone and to formulate it in some short sentences or words. You can help other older people find meaning in their lives by creating particular circumstances in which they will be able to discover and communicate about their values. Many people are unaware of the values that are guiding their lives. Creating the right circumstances can mean simply cultivating your willingness to listen — to have or to make time to listen to another older person. By expressing thoughts to someone who listens and by listening ourselves, we can discover the values that give meaning to our lives. By listening we can also help others seek values that will give them a deeper and more fulfilling sense of meaning.

Contemplation and meditation on our inner lives and our surrounding world will also help us discover meaningful values. This is not a quick or easy process. It sometimes takes a long time before you will find and accept values which will give meaning to your life.

In the rushing and the noise that are so characteristic of our society, people not only need leisure time but also time for contemplation and meditation in a quiet place. Relaxation, which seems ironically to have a more and more important place in our fast-paced world, is only a first step in the right direction. Relaxation is not an end in itself; it is a condition for beginning a meditative and contemplative approach to life.

Have your own "desert" where you can enjoy solitude and take refuge from overwork and noise. It takes courage to be alone with your thoughts. Many people are frightened by their own thoughts. If you cannot find solitude in your daily way of life, it would be good if you could have your own "portable desert" (*not* portable radio) where you *can* find solitude amid noisy surroundings — a place where you can discover creative, experiential, or attitudinal values.

Conscience Formation

Finding the meaning of life is a challenge. We have to choose to do this by following our own consciences. That is why the education of conscience is the most important part of the entire educational process.

The education of our children and young people has

to start with helping them educate and refine their consciences. It is possible for people to be wrong in their choices when their values are rooted in the quest for money, prestige, or appearance. Even so, it is preferable to live in a world where people have the right to make choices, even if they end up being wrong choices, rather than in a world where there are no choices at all. It is better to live in a world that permits both a Hitler and a Mother Teresa rather than a world where every human being is just a robot who follows the commands imposed by a party or dictator.

Review Your Own Life

Socrates said that the unexamined life is not worth living. It is important for older people to examine and, better yet, write about life's meaningful conclusion. This is what's meant by "life review." In their older age many people discover new aspects of life. Because they have known the breadths of existence, they are now ready to know its depths. Finding this meaning of life — the ultimate meaning — is a privilege of older age. Some of you may need encouragement to look for meaning. If this is true for you, try to see that choices always exist to the last day of life, so that you may face the final challenge with courage and dignity.

Academic literature on life review reveals that many psychologists and gerontologists (scientists who study aging and problems associated with it) identify the process of life review as an opportunity for the elderly to find meaning through autobiographical approaches.[13] Many psychologists agree that life review appears to be one of the developmental tasks of the last stage of life.

There is a sense of urgency for the elderly to share their life story. One of the developmental tasks of aging is to maintain a past-scanning function that reclaims the past. Our personal experiences are always located in time. The fear of forgetting and the need to remember both mark the last stage of life. Memory enables us to hold fast to our identity and to shape and interpret it in new ways. We do not merely have these memories; we are these memories. By remembering, we make connections and discover the patterns and designs of our lives and facilitate the next stage which includes death.[14]

The Meaning of Life: Real People's Stories

Mr. P. is a 90-year-old gentleman who is bedridden and requires oxygen most of the time. He suffers from emphysema and heart disease. He taught mathematics at a university for 29 years and was married to a "beautiful lady," as he calls her, for 53 years. She died nine years ago.

When asked what he had learned about life through his experiences of suffering, he responded, "One word says it; it is *patience*. If you just wait long enough, things will happen the right way." He had especially learned how to be patient when he was sick and had to rely on others to care for him at their pace. He finds much pleasure in visits from his daughter and a close friend who comes by occasionally. When asked about what gives meaning to his life now, he stated, "The Bible. One passage says it all…." He quoted John 3:16 saying, "For God so loved the world that he gave his only Son, so that everyone who believes in him might not perish but might have eternal life." When asked if he wanted to join his wife, Mr. P. said, "Oh, yes. In a way I had one foot in heaven for the 53 years I had her. I might as well get the other one there."

When asked about attitudes which had helped him find meaning in his life, he said, "The best way to get rid of an enemy is to make him your friend. That has helped me to have more friends and to learn more about people."

Mrs. L. is a ninety-year-old widow who has lived in a nursing home for about eight years. She was the youngest of five siblings but was born fourteen years after the next youngest sibling. Mrs. L.'s family expected her to stay home and take care of her mother, but she married as a teenager and had a daughter one year later and a son three years later. She worked in an office-supply business for six months but spent the remainder of her life raising her family and taking care of her mother. She described work at home as equally important to what women do today. She stated simply, "Work is work if you call it that. It's pleasure if you call it that."

She values prayer as most important in her life. She is a member of the Unity Church, which believes strongly in the union of the individual being with God. She stated she believed strongly in "being beautiful on the inside and presentable on the outside."

When dealing with difficult times of sickness and death, she said, "I might feel confused and fuzzy at first, but my next question will be: What should we do now?" She described a recent experience of acquiring over 80 signatures on a get-well card for a resident in the nursing home. She is a member of the resident council, which helps facilitate communication between the nursing home's residents and administrative personnel.

Miss T. is an 88-year-old woman who lives alone in an apartment. She was a pharmacist in a hospital for many years and has been retired since she was 69. She has no relatives who live in the area. When the weather is good, she is very active and often goes out for lunch or to shopping areas to run errands and get outside. She is a member of a large church and attends Sunday services, as well as Wednesday night services when transportation is available. She has been an active member of the Spinners and Weavers' Guild, serving as secretary for almost 20 years. She also attended this organization's annual conventions throughout the United States for 16 years. She states that she has never had any real setbacks in life except during the Great Depression and when her parents died. When they died, she realized that "life is short" and "death is inevitable." Miss T. feels that people learn most from the "down" years because "when we are living in the 'up' times we go gaily along, taking it all for granted and not giving enough thought to it to learn much from it. One thing which is not good is to look inward too much and to not associate enough with others to find out what is meaningful to them and what they expect from life." She adds, "Give serious thought to the meaning of life early in your life....Otherwise you may just drift along until it is too late to do much about it, and you will have lived your life with no purpose."

Mrs. M., a 77-year-old widow, lives in her own home. She has one son. She has been a beautician and still has a shop in her home. She is involved in several professional associations and church activities. Mrs. M. also volunteers in a nursing home, attends community concerts with friends, and does gardening. She believes that she is happy today and thinks that the best time in her life was when her husband was alive and her son was living at home. Meaning in life for Mrs. M. is to forget herself and do as much as she can for others. Earlier in life her meaning was focused more on her family. She is not certain that she would change her life if she were to relive it, but she might. If she could change her life now, she would like to hear better. She has had a hearing disability for about 40 years. She said that this causes her to misunderstand others and to be misunderstood. Her goals are to write children's stories, to put order in some photographs, to compile a book of her mother's poetry and stories, and to sort out her belongings and give them away. She said that material things are not as important now that she is older.

Mrs. H. is a 76-year-old widow and a resident of a nursing home. She has lived there for 10 years since a debilitating stroke. Prior to living in the nursing home, Mrs. H.'s life had been hard. She had lost two children to severe illnesses in their youth; another son committed suicide when he was forty; her husband died after a prolonged illness; another son left his wife and children, and no one has heard from him in over a year.

Mrs. H. has always been relatively poor and has known days of hunger. Our conversation revealed many tragic experiences in her life, but she gave the impression of someone who had risen above or "transcended" those sufferings. Through the interview it became apparent that this positive attitude came from her willingness to see the choices before her, to make a choice, and to accept responsibility for the choice she made. Mrs. H.

also commented several times on her "calling" at the nursing home — a calling to "serve other people, make others happy, be helpful, laugh, and see some humor in every day."

What *is* the meaning of life in older age? Here are some answers from older people themselves.

- "Growing older is what you make it. Be your age, but act like you feel. I don't feel any older this year than last. I have no complaints about this time in my life."
- "You have to have something to do, and that's what helps you. That's what helped me because I have to keep doing something. I can't sit and hold my hands, and that's why I try to tell the people here, they must not give up, because age doesn't mean anything. It's the way you feel inside, I think. There are a lot of people in their eighties who are doing beautiful work."
- "There is nothing good about growing older. It's better to be young and do what you want to do. Old age is what you make of it."
- "You have to have hope that something good will happen. I try not to be a pessimist. As I grow older, I have a sense of hope for better things to come."
- "I feel no real change in myself, except for some wrinkles. I look forward to the future with pleasure because I am freed from work pressures and the tyranny of time. I will have time to ponder, to relax, and to enjoy my family."

- "I enjoy good health, so I don't feel old, and I have no intention of playing that role. I'm retired but not 'put out to pasture.'"
- "If I could choose, I would like nine more lives just like this one. My life is in my hands, and I am in control of it....As far as I am concerned, my whole life has been filled! Oh, I have had ups and downs. I have had my concerns, but I have also been blessed. The Lord has been good to me all of my 74 years. I do not fear or dread old age; it is part of life."

Irvin Yalom, in his book *Existential Psychotherapy,* came to the following conclusions after reviewing results obtained from his research on the Purpose in Life test compiled by James Crumbaugh and Leonard Maholik and the Life Regard Index of John Battista and Richard Almond.[15] Yalom concluded that for all ages, old as well as young,

a. A lack of...meaning in life is associated with psychopathy in a linear sense. That means the less sense of meaning in life, the greater the severity of psychological problems in the person.
b. A positive sense of meaning in life is associated with deeply held religious beliefs, self-transcendent values (a person wants to be *better*...), membership in groups, dedication to some cause, [and] adoption of clear life goals.

Yalom also concluded that meaning of life must be viewed from a developmental perspective. This means that types of meaning may change over an individual's life. Values that give meaning at one time in life may not be as valuable at later life stages. In one period of life a person will find purpose through creative values. In another period, attitudinal or experiential values may give one's life its meaning.

Older People's Attitudes: A Survey

In order to find out what values older people in Omaha, Nebraska, held, I sent the Purpose in Life test (P.I.L.) to a sample group aged 60 and over. I asked each respondent to indicate personal age, sex, and living situation. Of the 130 people asked to respond, 60 percent completed and returned their forms.

Only 5 percent of the respondents felt that their lives had little meaning, while 63 percent of the subjects indicated that their lives had definite purpose and meaning. The remaining 32 percent fell in the "undecided" category.

People in the "old" elderly group (ages 73 to 95) scored significantly higher. That means that they found more meaning in life than those in the "young" elderly group (ages 60 to 72). The fact that P.I.L. scores were higher for the "old" elderly group is contrary to what people might expect. One explanation could be that the persons aged 60 to 72 were approaching retirement or had recently retired and thus were in a transition period in which they were still creating the alternative values needed to replace work as a primary source of life and meaning. The 73 to 95 group may have already adjusted to retirement and had developed other ways to find fulfillment in life. Another possible explanation is that those in the "old" elderly group have lived longer precisely *because* they have found meaning in their lives, while those who did not find such meaning died at an earlier age. It is also interesting to note that no significant difference was found between males and females and their levels of experiencing meaning in life.

With regard to living situations, the level of meaning did not seem to be influenced according to whether the person lived alone, with a spouse, with relatives, or in a home for older people. *How* older people view their living situation is more important than their living situation itself. Another finding from this research indicates that the values from which older people derive the most meaning in life are (1) family, (2) spiritual needs, (3) good health, (4) helping others, and (5) self-reliance.

Despite their emphasis on the importance of good health, many older people in the survey felt that illness and suffering could be blessings too. Illness and suffering were positive experiences for 30 percent of the sample group, and 25 percent said it was a neutral experience, saying things like "You have to make the best of it." This could indicate that many older people derive meaning in life through attitudinal values — by facing suffering with courage. Their suffering has the meaning of sacrifice. They see it as the will of God that ultimately will produce good fruits for themselves or their friends; they see it as part of their lives here on earth.

Creative values did not seem to be quite as important to the people in the survey. These values were not mentioned very frequently. Well-meaning people have put much money, time, and energy into helping the elderly engage in creative activities; however, this may not be the best approach in helping older people find meaning in their lives. The survey shows that experiential and attitudinal values seem to be more important.

The practical implications of the research suggest that people must learn to develop values other than work-oriented ones before they approach retirement. The capacity to enjoy the beauty of a sunset, to listen to good music, to read good literature, to enjoy paintings and other art, to love and be loved, or to derive some good from suffering should be learned at a younger age. Such activities will help a person have a more meaningful older age.

In reflecting on the interviews and the research with the Purpose in Life test, I have some problems with the view of Simone de Beauvoir in her book *The Coming of Age*. She defends an activist point of view of growing older as being the only way to escape an existential vacuum — a meaninglessness in older age: "The greatest good fortune, even greater than wealth, for the older person is to have his world still inhabited by projects; then, busy and useful, he escapes both from boredom and from decay...."[16]

Older age, in her view, is not a time for contemplation, for experiential values, for beauty in one's self, other people and nature, and for sharing of wisdom. Her view is often preached to the older generation as the only way to follow in order to have a good and graceful older age. It is certainly a product of our "doing" culture, which is the opposite of a "being" culture. In Western culture, what matters is what you *do* and not so much what you *are*, which puts the elderly in a disadvantaged position.

It's Up to You

If young people today hope to have a meaningful older age, they need to learn to respect and love older people. If the older generation is not an active part of their lives, they are likely to see no meaning of life in older age. They will then likely hate themselves when they are old because they can find no meaning and pride in their own old age.

Likewise, if we hope to have young people in our lives as we grow older, we must respect younger people too. If you don't yet know about the art of *listening* as well as talking, this is the time to learn. All high-quality relationships are based on *communication* — the give-and-take of mutual concern for each others' lives — that is the essence of love. Younger people do not necessarily "owe" us all their time and attention; we *all* owe one another active interest in one anothers' lives.

We all must help *other* older people to live a good life too — a life that is as meaningful and as long as possible. We must also help one another have a death that is as meaningful as possible. Sometimes a person's death can explain the meaning of his or her life. Life and death are not only meaningful for the dying people but also for others around them too. How many families have been reunited through the sickness or death of a father, mother, relative, or good friend?

There is something to discover in older age — an aspect of life which cannot be known before it. Older age is a time of fulfillment — a special time that the biblical writers called *kairos*. It can be the best time of life. It can help you take care of unfinished business with your own soul, with others, and with God.

Frankl's theory of life's meaning does not answer all the problems of aging or even attempt to explain them. As we grow older, we reflect on life's ups and downs. As we accept the certainty of death, the meaning of our lives will become more apparent and can, in turn, illuminate the meaning of our older age. The choices that created this life and its meanings are past. We cannot change them. But new choices exist. There is still time to choose our own way — to concentrate on the inner life and relationships with God and other people. There is still time to hold our heads high and courageously face whatever comes.

A general meaning of life seems difficult to conceive if we don't believe in a Supreme Being — a creator of the world and of life. If we discover a comprehensive meaning of our whole life, it will be the consequence of a step by step spiritual journey. Each step will have its meaning and will bring us closer to accepting the will of God. It will be an encounter with God through contemplation and meditation. We will seek the divine meaning in all that happened or will happen and try to find out what God expects of us so that we can respond by giving meaning to what we did and what we are doing every moment of our lives.

SOURCES

[1]Jean-Paul Sartre as cited in R. Hepburn's, "Questions About the Meaning of Life," *Religious Studies,* Vol. 1 (1965), pp. 125-140.

[2]Leo Tolstoy, *My Confession, My Religion: The Gospel in Brief* (New York: W.W. Norton, 1983), p. 20.

[3]*Ibid.* p. 12.

[4]Albert Camus as cited in A. Jaffe's, *The Myth of Meaning in the Work of C.G. Jung* (London: Hodden and Stroughton, 1970), title page.

[5]Albert Camus, *The Myth of Sisyphus and Other Stories* (New York: Random House, 1959), pp. 14-15.

[6]Carl G. Jung, *Collected Works,* Vol. 6, *The Practice of Psychotherapy* (New York: Pantheon, Bollinger Series, 1966), p. 83.

[7]Harold Kushner, *When All You've Ever Wanted Isn't Enough* (New York: Summit Books, 1987).

[8]Viktor Frankl, *Man's Search for Meaning: An Introduction to Logotherapy* (Boston: Beacon Press, 1985).

[9]Viktor Frankl, *The Doctor of the Soul: From Psychotherapy to Logotherapy* (New York: Alfred A. Knopf, 1965), p. XIII.

[10]Viktor Frankl, *Man's Search for Meaning...,* p. 178.

[11]*Ibid.,* p. 122.

[12]C.S. Lewis, *Surprised by Joy: The Shape of My Early Life* (New York: Harcourt Brace and World, 1956), pp. 16-18.

[13]B.J. Hateley, *Telling Your Story, Exploring Your Faith* (St. Louis, MO: Christian Board of Publication, 1985).

[14]Melvin A. Kimble, "Aging and the Search for Meaning" (unpublished paper presented at the Conference of Religion and Aging, Claremont, CA, in April 1987).

[15]Irvin D. Yalom, *Existential Psychotherapy* (New York: Basic Books, Inc., 1980), pp. 459-460.

[16]Simone de Beauvoir, *The Coming of Age*, trans. Patrick O'Brien (New York: G.P. Putnam and Sons, 1972), p. 492.

CHAPTER TWO

The Meaning of Suffering in Older Age

Suffering ceases to be when one finds a meaning for it.

Viktor Frankl

Reflecting on the meaning of suffering in general and the meaning of suffering for a particular individual is not an easy thing to do. In fact, a person who is suffering is the only one who knows what it means. Writing or speaking about suffering in older age also contradicts the media images of happy older people enjoying their retirement years, and most articles about older people are written to explain recent discoveries on how to age gracefully.

Suffering Is Normal

Suffering is, in fact, devalued by modern Western culture. We cling to a utopian ideal of living without pain, suffering, or death. Our generation could be called the "Valium generation" because we tend to look for the sedation of all pain — of all present and future sufferings. Yet, suffering is a real part of life, and it becomes more evident in older age when one has to cope with many physical and psychosocial losses. Older people also feel suffering more deeply because they are often isolated from their communities, friends, and relatives, and are lacking the physical strength to cope with that isolation.

We all suffer because we all are human beings knowing what it means to be happy. Happiness and suffering are like love and hate. They are not opposites; they are components of the same reality. Happiness always presumes the possibility of being able to suffer, and suffering can be the beginning of happiness. This is the reason that some people are afraid to love someone and be happy — because there is always suffering in the experience of being loved and of loving another person. Experiencing happiness today can create the fear that one day in the future we will lose that happiness and suffer from all kinds of physical or spiritual pain.

Some people purposely suffer by imposing on themselves great sacrifices in order to become happier. A mother suffers birth pains in order to give life. College students endure years of difficult studies in order to become more knowledgeable. People diet in order to become healthier and more attractive.

When we dream of a world without suffering, we often forget that suffering is a part of the history of humanity. The capacity to suffer has been and still is the origin of realizing and transcending our own human nature. If we were not able to suffer, we would be lifeless stones. We would not be able to create, invent, or be happy because surviving difficult circumstances and finding solutions to problems is the beginning of all human development. David Wendell Moller expressed this truth in the following way:

If humanity is deprived of the capacity to suffer then it embarks on a path which narrows the experience of being human. To be alive is to actively engage the world and others with the full complement of human responses, and this includes suffering. I am concerned that feelings, unlike behavioral activities, cannot be readily compartmentalized nor turned on and off. I would argue that the nullification of suffering diminishes one's ability to feel and hence affects the capacity to feel joy as well. To deny suffering is to eliminate meaningfulness of human experience from suffering. Living becomes the pursuit of endless satisfaction and pleasure, and life without suffering becomes a pseudo-experience — banal, trivial, and most important, unfulfilling.[1]

The Good to Be Found in Suffering

There are, in fact, many *positive* aspects to suffering. What kind of a world would it be if all suffering were eliminated, not only for ourselves but also for humanity as a whole? Arthur McGill described the positive value of suffering in the following way:

For instance, let us suppose that God might so interfere in situations that all our suffering would be immediately removed. At the first pain of hunger, for example, a meal would miraculously appear on the table. Upon cutting ourselves with a knife accidentally, we would be instantly healed. Upon being defrauded of our savings by some criminal, new money immediately appears in our possession. We can appreciate the problems which would arise in the "ideal" world. First, much of human creativity and striving are directed to the overcoming of some bit of suffering. Hunger has provoked us to develop hunting skills and agricultural techniques. Against disease we have fostered medicine. The moral patterns we adopt warn us against sufferings which we may produce in the lives of others. In any deep human relationships we discover how essential it is that the other rebuke and correct us at certain points.

A real relationship always involves the suffering experience of being judged. What is love that does not judge? It does not love us. It simply humors us.[2]

We all have our crosses to carry. Sometimes we are so busy carrying our own crosses that we forget to look around us to see how others are carrying *their* crosses. So many times we simply do not see the burdens of others we meet. Focusing on only the glittering aspects of a fellow human being's life blinds us to see the other not-so-happy aspects.

No one is without pain or problems. People who think they lack pain will often create it or worry about the fact that they do not have any immediate problem or pain. Our suffering can be real or it can be imagined, and imagined suffering is sometimes the worst kind.

Suffering can be explained by circumstances, or it can be a consequence of what we have done to ourselves. Sometimes it comes to good and generous people without warning and without any explanations. Why bad things happen to good people and good things happen to bad people is a question we hear throughout life. No age group (including teenagers and older people) has a corner on the supply of suffering; *everyone* suffers in different degrees and at different moments. Suffering happens when we are born, when we are growing up, when we are adults, and when we are older.

A Unique Task Rooted in Love

Viktor Frankl's book *Man's Search for Meaning*[3] has sold more than two million copies and has been translated into many languages. It has touched the hearts of millions who have sought meaning in their sufferings. As a concentration camp survivor from World War II, Frankl knew what it meant to suffer and to endure the horrible suffering of his fellow prisoners. In his book he shows us that it is possible to grow…even in a concentration camp. Frankl reminds us that when we find it is our destiny to suffer, we must see our suffering as a task — a unique task — that no one else can do for us. We must accept the fact that even in our suffering we are unique.

No one can and will ever be able to understand your suffering completely, and no one can relieve you from all your suffering. But in the same way no one will be able to bear your burden as you are willing to bear it. Being alone with suffering gives people the opportunity of being unique in the way that they face their own personal distresses.

Suffering totally oppresses some people. They may tell us, "It is too much.…" The only thing we can do in such circumstances is *cum pati* — suffer with them, as the Latin words signify. On the other hand, some suffering people are an inspiration for others. We don't have to go to them in order to help them, they help us. Their attitude is not a stoic one. They do not stay above their own painful situation, but they are instead immersed *in* their suffering, and they talk to us in an inspiring way from inside their own suffering.

No animal can do what a human being is able to do — to survive the most painful situations, not just because we want to survive or somehow "prove" ourselves but because we love someone and someone loves us. A mother and son living in the same house may feel alienated and isolated from each other while a husband and wife separated by an ocean feel extremely close. That's because they love each other. An ocean and distances cannot prevent that husband and wife from feeling close to each other. The suffering of being far away may even create a deeper love relationship.

French author and aviator Antoine de Saint-Exupery once lost his way while flying through a blizzard in the Andes. The bad conditions forced him to land his small plane. He started to walk, although he did not know in what direction he was going. He could not imagine how far he was from other living beings. He did not know if he would make it. He had nothing to eat or drink. When his shoes wore out, he threw them away. Frostbite set into his feet, and he started to grow tired. Hunger and thirst joined him, and he then began to wonder if it would not be better to lie down in the snow and never wake up again. But at that same moment he thought of his wife. She waited for him back home. He knew that if he would give up and die there in the snow, his wife would never experience the happiness of his homecoming after such a long time. He knew that his wife was probably thinking: "If he lives, he is certainly coming in my direction, he is flying, or walking, toward me." That kept him going through this blizzard. "If he lives, he walks toward me, because he loves me. If he lives, he walks. If he lives, he walks." Repeating these words over and over again, Saint-Exupery continued to walk until he fell unconscious in the snow and later woke up in a small hospital. Because of his wife who waited for him and whom he really loved, he survived.

Martin Gray is another example of a person who went through a lot of sufferings. As a child he lived in a Warsaw ghetto during World War II. From the age of 14 he was marked for extermination by the Germans. They forced him to wear an armband emblazoned with the Star of David, which identified him as a Jew. He chose, however, to fight the Nazis rather than passively accept his fate. He risked his life to smuggle food to his mother and brothers who hid behind a false cupboard in their Warsaw apartment. When the members of his family were betrayed and herded aboard a train for the infamous Treblinka concentration camp, Martin Gray joined them in a rescue attempt. When he realized that they had been murdered, he escaped and became active in the Polish resistance movement against the Nazis. He constantly envisioned the day when he would overcome the Nazis and avenge his family's deaths. When at last he marched victoriously into Berlin as an officer of the Russian army, he realized:

My revenge was bitter. I could sense the fear around me, those lines of men and women waiting for a little water, and who suddenly froze, went silent, because I was passing. I too had lined up for a little water on the banks of the Vistula; I too had seen a uniformed stranger, who was absolute power and the new law, walk up to me. Old women in black, motionless, holding containers, men stooping over ruins, I know you. I know you, dead city, hungry and frightened, I know how to tell the victims from the butchers. They hit us first, and you let it happen, then they pushed you in front, like a shield. Today it's your turn. And we have butchers too.[4]

Gray recognized the suffering of the Germans because it mirrored his own suffering. The conflict between compassion and revenge raged inside him. Where would he find the solution to the conflict between good and evil, light and dark, peace and bitterness, love and hate? Perhaps he was referring to this when he wrote,

"Man has two roads always before him. And he must choose between them. Two roads before his eyes, two destinies. And at each step there is a new crossing. Two roads, two possible destinies. And he will travel so until the last second of his life."[5]

While struggling with that conflict, he remembered his mother. Her love gave him strength in his suffering. She was a very gentle, quiet person who had no need to speak, for all her acts were full of love. When he entered the first enemy town, ready to avenge his family's murders, his mother's image held him back.

When he and his fellow soldiers searched the town for the enemy, they found only the very old and the very young. Many other Russian soldiers completed the cycle of destruction begun by the Germans. They killed indiscriminately. While carrying out one of these searches, Gray came to a turning point in his quest for meaning.

A child turned back toward the door of a cellar, his face was covered with tears. He wiped his nose with the back of his hand. He was waiting for someone to appear. An old woman came out, bent double by age — no doubt his grandmother. Reaching out her hand to him she drew him to her, caressing his face as he buried himself in her black pleated skirt. This hand on a child's cheek; it was my mother with me. I shouted out an order. My comrades looked at me, shrugging their shoulders and spitting toward the inhabitants as they moved off. I was the last to leave, turning around to see this old woman and child, one against the other. My dead mother had saved me from the violent part of myself. Her gentleness and goodness had prevented me from letting it prevail over me.[6]

During these difficult times Gray lived for those he loved. The thought of his family gave him life. He knew that he could not succeed in avenging his family's murders completely because they would never be restored to life. That is the failure of revenge. Death cannot be redeemed. Gray believed that only another life can erase death. His philosophy of life in the face of suffering is perhaps best expressed in the following passage:

Cold reason is not enough for man. It is merely the soil that must have water to germinate. The water is love, is others, is the hope and the belief that tomorrow, in each man and first of all one's self, the fresh and beautiful will have sprung up. [There is] the certainty that man will be able to live in peace and joy, with himself and others. And if suffering comes, and it will come since death will always be there, [there is] the hope that man will take this suffering into his hands and make it a fruit [—] to derive from it the certainty that one must live a higher, better life, in [the] fragile miracle which is life.[7]

Stoics try to remain above suffering — to make an abstraction of it. Responsible human beings use their suffering to prove that they love others. To suffer is to dedicate yourself to other human beings. For example, scientists do not do research for its own sake, but because people are waiting for the results which may help make them better, happier, healthier, or more knowledgeable. Researchers will make sacrifices and suffer in order to help people. If people work hard for a business, suffer to build up a program, burn the midnight oil to write a book, or strive to be a good teacher, they often do it because other people will have a better life as a result. If they do it only for fame or money, the work and suffering may be destructive in themselves. Suffering must be linked to other people; its results must be shared with and for others in order to be human.

The same is true for happiness. Happiness is essentially being happy with and for others. The others will give more meaning to our own happiness, just as they will give more meaning to our own suffering.

The Categories of Suffering

There are different kinds of suffering which may be experienced in various ways and degrees.

First, there is *physical* suffering. You can suffer physically from an illness, an injury, a tumor, from cold and heat, or from fatigue and sleeplessness. Having a leg amputated, experiencing a stroke, becoming partially paralyzed, losing eyesight, or suffering from multiple sclerosis — these are all difficult crosses to bear.

Another kind of suffering is *emotional* suffering. It may be caused by the death of a loved one, rejection by a peer group, dissatisfaction with a job or lifestyle, or by loneliness. Familial, marital, and mental problems or worries about the past or the future may create deep sufferings that cannot be measured by objective standards or compared to others' problems.

Spiritual suffering is the third kind of suffering. It is the feeling we get when it seems that our lives are out of touch with God or that we no longer have faith in God. It's also the kind of suffering we experience when we feel our mortality or fear that we are damned or great sinners.

All these different kinds of suffering vary from person to person. They even vary within a single individual at different times and under different circumstances. But all these types of suffering are interrelated and influence one another. Spiritual or emotional suffering is usually an element of each incident of physical suffering we experience. A person who loses his leg in an accident will suffer from it emotionally. He feels that he is not accepted by society. He may blame God for his loss and be angry that something so terrible happened to him for no reason. Why is it that so many bad things can happen to good people who did everything possible to obey God and the Church? Why is it that so many good things happen to bad people?

Everyone who suffers does not react in a negative way to their fate. Some people give us an example of acceptance, courage, and inspiration.

George was a sick older man. He had diabetes, and both his legs had been amputated. His eyesight was severely impaired. He loved to talk about his experiences as General Patton's assistant. Although physically disabled, his clear mind could recount history in the making. This once very powerful person had to be fed by a nurse, and someone had to wipe his chin when he spilled his soup. All that he had left was there in his room — several pictures of his family, a watch pinned to his gown so he could see the time, a chair from home strewn with several handmade pillows, and an afghan that the Veterans of Foreign Wars had given him. George had given all his war medals and honors to his nephews when he moved into the nursing home. He said that he enjoyed their visits but because they lived out of town, they could not come very often.

Although he had been through so much, George continued to set goals. His next goal was to get his diabetes under control and visit his nephew's home for Christmas. Not one word of complaint came from his lips. He was making plans to fight his illness in a systematic way and was full of hope and courage. He was an inspiration for the nursing home residents and staff.

Loretta was an elderly bedridden woman who did not recognize her own children. She talked of her husband who had been dead for 25 years as if he were still living. Loretta would tell her husband to "let the dog out." Deep pain and suffering filled Loretta's son when his mother couldn't put herself in the proper time and place or when she uttered unintelligible sounds and groans. Loretta's room was sparsely furnished. It seemed incredible that one could place a lifetime of possessions into one small room. Most of her life's memories stood by in the form of pictures. The helplessness of Loretta's son put my own sufferings in another perspective. To be in contact with the sufferings of other people can assist us in seeing our own sufferings in a more objective, relative way.

Many say that sickness and misfortune change people's personalities, that people become totally different when they endure suffering. Some people who were healthy and happy become angry and negative after a misfortune. Others don't.

David was a difficult and very aggressive young man who became a gentle, caring "housefather" after the birth of his handicapped child. It can be true that suffering changes a personality, but the opposite can also be true — sickness and suffering sometimes reveal our basic personality, which differs from the masks we are used to wearing. We all sometimes wear masks to conceal our basic personality from others and also from ourselves. Some of us are superb actors. Too often we judge ourselves by the acting role we play and not by our real selves. We go through life as robots. Robots don't interact with one another. We often just act in the roles of father, mother, husband, wife, teacher, waiter, doctor, lawyer, or priest. We may mostly be the person that we are supposed to be in a particular role, at a particular time. How frightened we are, then, when one day we come in contact with ourselves and with another real human being!

The Meaning of Unavoidable Suffering

The meaning of *all* suffering doesn't exist. A general and universal meaning applicable to all kinds of suffering is impossible to formulate. Suffering is always very personal and, therefore, unique. Your suffering cannot be compared with the suffering of another human being because suffering is very subjective. Someone will suffer more from a financial misfortune than another person will from the death of an only child.

If each person's suffering is unique, then the meaning of your suffering will be unique too. This meaning relates to the psychology of the suffering person, to the circumstances, the time, and the kind of event which caused it. Some suffering may be more readily accepted as a part of being an older person than if it had come in an earlier stage of life. People who have never suffered or have never been in contact with suffering during childhood and adolescence will have more problems finding meaning when they suffer as adults or older persons. They will also be inclined to exaggerate their conditions. A person without friends, a person without deep faith in God, or a lonely person will have more difficulty in coping with sufferings and misfortunes. All people must learn *how* to suffer when they are younger. Suffering is a lifelong learning process that begins the day we are born. This does not mean that we will be able to carry our crosses without flinching or feeling pain, but this learning process will help us carry our crosses better than other people who avoid the school of suffering. For this reason it's best not to protect children too much. Providing a totally carefree existence for youngsters leaves them ill-prepared for real life because real life will not always be easy. There will be problems...for *everyone*. Just as people must learn to love, they must learn to suffer. Coping with a little pain in a positive way helps us cope with greater suffering in other circumstances. Bad experiences are not utterly worthless as long as we learn from them.

There is an inherent contradiction in the phenomenon of suffering. We need suffering, in a certain measure, to become adults. On the other hand, suffering and pain are repulsive to our human existence. It is a fact that the most beautiful human beings have gone through quite a bit of suffering — suffering which they have digested and in which they have found meaning. To be in a crisis, to go through suffering and pain, is often a strong foundation needed to become more human.

How much pain can a person bear? Some people are surprised at their own inner forces and coping mechanisms. Hope and faith offered through the helping hands of a friend can also work miracles. Human beings measure the worth of life through events which either bring pain or pleasure. If something is pleasing and happy, it is "good"; if it causes hardship and pain, it is labeled "bad." Such designations are not always true. Often the most unpleasant things are richest in their compensations. Hard times can give your life the richest harvest. Only time and patience can help you discover this truth.

Finding meaning in suffering is a difficult and energy-draining process. It has different stages: shock, denial, anger, depression, and ups and downs. Then after a certain turning point, you will see some light at the end of the tunnel.

That turning point can come when you meet another person who is willing to go that extra mile with you in your way of the cross. It could also be a particular circumstance, for example, reading the Bible or a good book. Finding meaning in suffering almost always presents itself after a dark period of time, first in a vague form which then becomes more concrete every time you talk about it and try to formulate it. This meaning or purpose will be a growing force that will become stronger and more deeply useful as time goes by.

"I had to believe," said a 35-year-old patient with multiple sclerosis, "that everything that happens in life happens for a purpose. Everything has a purpose and is meant for our good. I was a popular guy, loving cars and girls, and confident of making a lot of money. The discovery of my illness changed my life. God taught me a lesson. He made me more thoughtful, more sensitive to others. Before that, I never worried about others. God has purged me of my pride and arrogance. He made me better."

Finding meaning in suffering is a combination of effort and chance, or *grace*. If you want to find meaning in a painful circumstance, you must try at first to survive and to come out of the depressing situation. If you are not trying to do it, nobody can do it in your place. But if you are trying to do it, the grace of God will help you come out of the dark tunnel of suffering. These two factors, *grace* and *human effort,* will help you cope with and digest the suffering in a positive spirit.

Grace is always amazing. This amazing grace is connected with what God's role is in our lives. The presence of the Holy Spirit in the life of each of us will push us to believe in God's grace and miracles. It is then that we may feel like Moses in the presence of the burning bush which told him, "Remove the sandals from your feet, for the place where you stand is holy ground" (Exodus 3:5).

The meaning of suffering is not found as a response to questions like "Why?" and "Why me and not someone else?" No one can explain why a person has to suffer some particular misfortune. The meaning of suffering is found in the existential answers to the questions: "What can I do with it?" "What can I make from the situation in which I find myself?"

The death of a child was, for a young woman, the start of a meaningful life, a life full of generosity to the poorest of the poor in Africa. For another person the sufferings of a divorce helped her to be more herself and to believe more in herself. We all have learned to appreciate one another more through the death of a common friend. We all have learned not to take one another for granted when a relative or friend is dying. It might sound trite but as the gift-shop poster says, "When life hands you lemons, make lemonade." Many people waste life's most important gifts when, in self-pity, they insist on continuing to ask "Why?"

What you see as a positive value in your sufferings is always very personal and unique. It may also be extremely inspirational for others.

When Marilyn's only child died, a couple whose child had died years earlier spent much quiet time with her at the funeral home. The silent presence of that couple did more for Marilyn than all the words that priests and friends offered trying to help her find meaning in such a tragedy.

The best attitude we can have in the face of suffering

is a *silent* presence. This silence — just *being* with the other — will be the beginning of a healing process that will take its time. God's presence manifests itself mostly in silence through the grace of peace. Everything we suffer can have value and can produce good fruits, if not for ourselves then for others.

Through their faith, Christians have a particular way of finding meaning in their sufferings. Christians believe in providence rather than fate. They believe that by doing God's will they ultimately will be blessed. Their faith teaches them that they participate in Christ's sufferings for the salvation of the world. They believe that through their sufferings here on earth they will have a better existence in the life hereafter.

In contemplating on the Cross of Jesus, you have a model of how to suffer, and this divine example can help you find meaning in suffering.

Saint Paul wrote that we have to provide our little share of the sufferings of Christ in order to help save all human beings: "Now I rejoice in my sufferings for your sake" (Colossians 1:24).

Questioning Why We Suffer: A Recent Phenomenon

In the theological works of Augustine, Thomas Aquinas, Ignatius of Loyola, and Martin Luther there is no mention of the problem of suffering as we see it today.

Suffering seemed to be accepted in that time as a part of life. It was not a problem; it had been taught in the Bible since the beginning of humankind that we are surrounded by the voices of suffering. Christians were then seen as "homeless people" in a secular world — always on an exodus, enduring the demands of hope and uttering the cries of suffering because their final destination was heaven, and earthly life was only a passage.

We Christians must understand that it is through suffering that our lives are redeemed. It is psychologically true that after some great and painful struggle one usually finds the deepest peace. Would that not be the same for Christians after our life here on earth?

Suffering can bring Christians closer together. Therefore, it should not seem unusual to find Christian people together at the foot of the Cross as they seek meaning. Many black spirituals reflect the acceptance of suffering as God's mysterious will. At the same time they exhibit confidence in the ultimate triumph of justice, truth, peace, and faith with words like:

Oh freedom, I love thee!
And before I'll be a slave
I'll be buried in my grave
And go home to my Lord and be free.

The Book of Job gives us the best approach, enabling us to find meaning in life throughout our sufferings.

When Job was silent and stopped scolding God, he started to see the beauty and the mystery of nature around him. He saw that a marvelous creation surrounded him and that God was good after all. Job understood that knowing and accepting God was more important than trying to find answers which no human being can or could ever give.

The meaning of suffering and the meaning of life are aspects of the same human reality. One aspect adds to the dimension of the other. Without suffering, without crises and problems, many people will never discover the meaning of their own lives or even catch glimpses of some provisional meaning in their day-to-day living. Without things like meaning of life, values and faith in God, faith in ourselves and in other human beings, no one will ever be able to detect meaning in suffering.

Everything valuable and dear to us grows slowly. It always takes time and patience to realize something good and strong. Everything has its own *kairos* — its own "God time." There is a time to live, there is a time to die, there is a time to suffer, there is a time to enjoy. But we like to forget that there is a time for suffering too. You will discover this time if you are patient with yourself, others, and God.

Be patient toward all that is unresolved in your heart. Try to love the questions themselves. Do not seek the answers which cannot be given, because you will not be able to live them. And the point is to live everything. Live the questions now. Perhaps you will then gradually without noticing it live along some distant day into the answers.[8]

There is no gathering of roses without being pricked by thorns. We must not try to eliminate the thorns because then there will never be roses. What counts in suffering is not so much the suffering but our attitude toward it. Suffering often cannot be eliminated or changed, but our *attitude* toward it can be.

Your *reaction* to suffering, not the suffering itself, will make you a witness for or against God. If suffering makes you bitter and creates hard feelings against God or others, you make God or loved ones responsible for your own unhappiness. In the final analysis, you must translate questions about the meaning of suffering into questions that ask how you will respond — what you intend to *do* with your suffering for yourself, others, and God. Every joy, but also every pain, is a miracle.

Rabbi Harold Kushner reflected on suffering the following way:

Are you capable of forgiving and accepting in love a world which has disappointed you by not being perfect, a world in which there is so much unfairness and cruelty, disease, crime, earthquakes, and accidents? Can you forgive its imperfections and love it because it is capable of containing great beauty and goodness, and because it is the only world we have?

Are you capable of forgiving and loving the people around you, even if they have hurt you or let you down by not being perfect? Can you forgive them and love them, because there aren't any perfect people around, and because the penalty for not being able to love imperfect people is condemning one's self to loneliness?

Are you capable of forgiving and loving God even when you have found out that He is not perfect, even when He has let you down and disappointed you by permitting bad luck and sickness and cruelty in His world, and permitting some of those things to happen to you? Can you learn to love and forgive Him despite His limitations, as Job does, and as you once learned to forgive and love your parents even though they were not as wise, as strong, or as perfect as you needed them to be?

And if you can do these things, will you be able to recognize that the ability to forgive and the ability to love are the weapons God has given us to enable us to live fully, bravely, and meaningfully in this less-than-perfect world?[9]

Suffering: A Christian Mystery

With the help of our Christian faith we know that when we experience suffering and darkness, God is with us. God's presence does not eliminate the suffering but helps us cultivate the right attitude toward the things we cannot change in life. The prophet Micah said, "Though I sit in darkness, the LORD is my light" (Micah 7:8). Job testified, "While he kept his lamp shining above my head… by his light I walked through darkness" (Job 29:3).

Suffering is and will always be a mystery — a dark forest. You don't explain a mystery, you respect it and trust God with it. Suffering could be an instrument for personal and spiritual growth and not necessarily an evil. On the other hand, much suffering results from the fact that all human beings are bound together with one another in an interdependence typical of our cosmos. My suffering is always linked to others and could have its redeeming place in the salvation of the world, just as the suffering of others could have a "miraculous" presence in my life. Above all we have to understand that God is love — a companion who participates and helps us in the creation of our own personality and of the world. Christ never promised us an easy life without suffering, but he promised us that we will never be alone in the painful times of life. His example on earth and his doctrine will help us find meaning and courage to bear our crosses.

We have to stop questioning why we suffer and, instead, let the suffering question *us* so that we can answer it by the way we face life. No one is more inspiring than a person who knows how to suffer. No one is a better light for others than when that light comes out of the darkness.

SOURCES

[1]David Wendell Moller, "On the Value of Suffering in the Shadow of Death," *Loss, Grief, and Care: A Journal of Professional Practice,* Vol. 1½ (Fall 1986, Winter 1986-87), p. 129.

[2]Arthur McGill, "Human Suffering and the Passion of Christ," in Flavian Dougherty's *The Meaning of Human Suffering* (New York: Human Science Press, 1982), pp. 160-161.

[3]Viktor E. Frankl, *Man's Search for Meaning* (Boston: Beacon Press, 1985).

[4]Martin Gray, *For Those I Loved* (Boston: Little, Brown & Co., 1972), p. 252.

[5]Martin Gray, *A Book of Life* (New York: Seabury Press, 1975), p. 201.

[6]*Ibid.* pp. 43-44.

[7]*Ibid.* p. 209.

[8]Rainer Maria Rilke, *Letters to a Young Poet* (New York: W.W. Norton and Co., 1963), p. 35.

[9]Harold S. Kushner, *When Bad Things Happen to Good People* (New York: Schocken Books, 1981), pp. 147-148.

CHAPTER THREE

Reflections on Christian Spirituality in Older Age

To know how to grow old is the master-work of wisdom.

Henri-Frédéric Amiel

According to *Webster's Collegiate Dictionary*, *spiritual* means (1) relating to or consisting of or affecting the spirit, (2) relating to sacred matters, (3) concerned with religious values, and (4) relating to supernatural beings or phenomena.[1] In other words, *spiritual* has to do with the spirit, with religion, and with supernatural phenomena. The term *spirituality* is defined by Webster as sensitivity or attachment to religious values, as the quality of being spiritual and, in ecclesiastical law, something that belongs to the Church or to a cleric.

In fact the words *spiritual* and *spirituality* have many interpretations. Fundamentally, they have a religious or supernatural aspect of being bound together with God or a so-called "vital force." Spirituality has an aspect that cannot be explained scientifically because it belongs to the supernatural world. All of these interpretations are important. Some people accept one of these aspects by equating spirituality and religion, while others associate spirituality only with supernatural matters.

The terms have another more basic aspect which is illuminated in such contemporary literature as the works of Viktor Frankl and Arden Barden. Their writing focuses on people's search for meaning in their relationships with God, self, other human beings, and nature. Spirituality is in this way connected to both meaningful relationships with others and with our inner selves.

"Spirituality may be defined as the realm of inner-human, interhuman, and beyond-human dynamics which integrates and gives meaning to all of human experience," wrote Barden.[2] Frankl concluded that the prisoners in concentration camps who survived the most difficult situations of the Holocaust were people who had found a definite meaning in their survival and life.[3]

The Search for Spirituality

In order to become spiritual human beings, we must seek and find meaning in both life in general and in the many particular events of daily life where God, nature, fellow human beings, and ourselves are involved. These provisional meanings that we may find in daily events are glimpses of an ultimate meaning. Working on a project, suddenly realizing beauty or God's presence, sensing momentary deep inner peace, or longing for beauty and love are examples of the search for provisional meanings which will help us find the ultimate meaning of our lives.[4] This search for meaning or meanings is an expression of the spiritual dimension of each human being, and it separates us from the animal world.[5]

There are also particular types of spirituality, like those of Saints Francis, Benedict, or Augustine that are practiced today in religious orders founded by these men. These saints created spiritualities linked to particular cultures and times, and their spirits continue to live today in ways of life followed and interpreted by their disciples. But what about our times? Is there a typical modern spirituality?

Contemporary Culture
Plays a Big Part

We can only speak of a modern spirituality if we can talk about a typical, well-defined culture of modern times. A culture is a unity and an interaction between the different domains of the human and technical sciences, between philosophies, arts, sciences, psychosocial phenomena, and religious beliefs. It is difficult, if not impossible, to speak about a specific spirituality where there is no well-defined particular culture, because spirituality develops within a culture and interacts with it. To formulate the principles of a modern spirituality, you must have a clear understanding of modern culture.[6]

Culture and spirituality have many things in common, but spirituality is always geared to critical reflections within a specific cultural context. Spirituality is not only a child of its culture but is also a critical approach toward certain attitudes of that culture when its people seek expressions of genuine faith in a supernatural being, in nature, in other human beings, and in themselves. An example of this critical reflection is given by W. Paul Jones:

This awareness had its inception while I was living in a Trappist monastery. It was there that I became aware of a way of life radically different from the one supremely valued by our society. And it was there I began to recognize this alternative way of life as one to which an elderly life-style may prophetically point. Thomas Merton provided the clue when he said, "One becomes a person of spirit only when she/he can do nothing and feel no guilt."...I still remember when I first sensed how all of this seemed to relate. On that day I wrote in my monastic journal this entry:

"The Trappist monks are subversives, not so much for what they say or think, but for what they are....In the midst of a culture of noise they choose silence; in a culture of work they choose contemplation; in a culture of self-realization they denounce the self; in a culture of achievement they declare that the winner will be loser and only the loser, winner; in a culture whose economy is utterly dependent on consumption, they insist upon detachment; in a culture intoxicated by facts and education, they insist upon ignorance as the basis of wisdom; in a culture of complexity they call us to simplicity of willing one thing; in a culture intent on a high standard of living they insist on a high standard of life."[7]

It is typical in our modern times to reflect on, analyze, and be rational about spirituality. In contrast with other spirituality forms of earlier times, today we want to create a modern spirituality that has to account for its origins and tell us where we are going. We want to know the content of our spirituality and be assured that it makes sense. Through statistics and questionnaires we like to see the profile of our spirituality and then change, add, or eliminate as is necessary to come to an ideal of modern spirituality.

Spirituality: An Art, Not a Science

In the early Christian times and in the Middle Ages, spirituality grew without research — it simply developed. People lived it and were not preoccupied with analyzing the values and creating profiles. In fact, it is difficult to measure our spiritual lives. We can ask ourselves questions like, "Where am I on a spiritual level? Am I better or worse than before?" When anyone looks back over life, there are as many reasons for pessimism as there are for optimism. It is not easy to measure one's spiritual level and compare it with any other moment, year, or stage in one's life. As older persons, we should not measure our own degrees of being spiritual and compare them with last year or when we were 30 or 20. As Saint Paul wrote, "When I was a child, I used to talk as a child, think as a child...." (1 Corinthians 13:11).

But do we really have to measure? Do we have to know how many degrees we are better or worse? To live a spiritual life, we must, as Henri Nouwen said, "Just find the courage to enter into the desert of our loneliness and to change it by gentle and persistent efforts into a garden of solitude."[8] The realm of spirituality is a dynamic place where we move from one end to the other, deeper or higher, without knowing exactly where we are. We are uniting ourselves with God, the vital force, or living within God, and it does not matter whether we can calculate our exact location in that garden of solitude.

Spirituality is a dimension that cannot be separated from the biological, psychological, social, material, and religious aspects of life. Life is interaction — the interplay of the different parts. No part can exist by itself, including the spiritual part. Our spiritual needs are connected with and influence our psychosocial, biological, and religious (whether private or organized) aspects of life. In our Western approach to reality, we always want to make distinctions and separations of entities. As followers of Aristotle, we are inclined to take a dualistic approach to reality. We divide things and phenomena into opposites like body and soul, material and spiritual, black and white, liberals and conservatives, Christians and pagans, day and night. That splitting of reality doesn't happen in many other cultures. For example, most Africans make no distinction between religion and other aspects of life, be they social, biological, material, or psychological. Everything is religion, as John Mbiti has illustrated:

Because traditional religions permeate all the departments of life, there is no formal distinction between the sacred and the secular, between the religious and nonreligious, between the spiritual and the material areas of life. Wherever the African is, there is religion: He carries it to the fields where he is sowing seeds or harvesting a new crop; he takes it with him to the beer party or to attend a funeral ceremony, and if he is educated, he takes religion with him to the examination room at school or in the university; if he is a politician he takes it to the house of parliament.[9]

The meaning of the term *spiritual* is broader than that of the word *religious*. Spiritual has to do with things beyond material phenomena. Listening to music, reading or writing literature, knowing and understanding, enjoying a sunset, admiring a painting, praying and meditating, singing, living, and loving are all parts of our spiritual lives. They give us not only joy but also meaning in coping with losses, with sinful behavior, and with suffering and death.

The relationship between the religious and the spiritual is also not always good, just as people's relationships with certain kinds of music and certain kinds of love are not always good for spiritual growth. Even religion can sometimes block or destroy one's spiritual growth. For example, Jesus criticized some Pharisees for obeying the letter of the law and not its spirit when he said, "This people honors me with their lips, but their hearts are far from me" (Matthew 15:8). Observing only the letter of a religious law can kill our spiritual lives.

Contemporary Styles of Christian Spirituality

Four fundamental trends are apparent in today's Christian spirituality. They are evident in Christian behavior and literature. These trends also differ from those expressed in other periods of history. They are in fact consequences of critical reflections and behavior in our modern culture.

1) Christian spirituality today responds to life — to its beauty and its injustices — and leads to action. This response is reflected in a person's prayers. Prayer is a response to life which takes place during enjoyment of beauty (mysticism) or in actively fighting injustice and evil. Unlike centuries ago, today prayer is no longer solely a withdrawal from the world or a reciting of psalms and formulas. Prayer also realizes people's union with God through beauty and through the cry for justice. This union with God invites Christians to experience all aspects of life.

2) Christian spirituality today looks to the universe. Today the whole world must be part of our existence. People suffer and are hungry in India, Africa, Latin America, and many other areas. These people are part of *our* world. The center of our prayer and action is no longer only our personal needs or needs of relatives and close friends or just the needs of our own country but the whole needy world.

3) Christian spirituality today is responsive and responsible to the poor. By listening to the poor, people today are listening to God. That is the theme of many Latin American liberation theologians' writing such as that of Helder Camara.[10] Authentic Christian spiritual life suggests that the poor are not just recipients of charity, but that they have a significant voice in the interpretation of the gospel. From the shepherds at Jesus' birth to his apostles, the poor were the first recipients of Christ's doctrine and the first proclaimers of the gospel.

4) Christian spirituality today is socially oriented. Not only our personal lives but also the society in which we live is important in our relationship with God. God relates not just to individuals but also to societies and to creation as a whole. The holocaust theme of our nuclear age underlies the many kinds of spirituality evident today. Through the dangerous and hopeful events of the culture in which you live, God invites you to save not just yourself but the human race as a whole.

These four fundamental trends also influence a contemporary Christian spirituality of older age. In order to talk about a Christian spirituality of older age in our time, we must understand that no stage in spiritual life is the final stage. We can always advance to the next stage. Our positive possibility thinking is able to create new stages and new horizons. These stages are all preparations for a life in which we will be totally united with God — the supernatural force of the universe. The physical limitations of older age can help us refine our visions of beauty and values. In that way we can find beauty and values that will give more meaning to the later years of life.

How to Develop Your Christian Spirituality in Older Age

- Work toward the causes of justice, peace, and environmental protection on local, national, and international levels.
- Create deeper bonds of love for God.
- Help provide for the spiritual and material needs of people.
- Develop your own spiritual life through prayer, reading, meditation, artistic creation, and enjoyment of the beauty of nature and other people.

Through such commitments, you will not only achieve your full potential but will also go beyond yourself for greater causes.[11] This self-transcendence can lead you out of "me-ness" — out of worries about diet, sleep, and exercise patterns. Thus enabled, you can do something for future generations. "Through children, through contributions to the culture, through friendships — these are ways in which human beings can achieve enduring significance for their actions which go beyond the limit of their own skins and their own lives."[12]

Think about it; don't *you* want future generations to remember you for helping preserve nature and for working to establish a just and nonracist society so that future generations could have a better life? You can help do this with both your prayers and actions. Your prayers can respond to *life*, reflecting its joy in nature, people, and God. Prayers may also become a source of courage in your fight against the injustice and hatred in the world. In both approaches you will realize your union *with* God and your life *in* God.

Authentic Christian spiritual life suggests that responding to the material and spiritual needs of the poor helps us come closer to the love and knowledge of God. "Because he dispensed justice to the weak and the poor, it went well with him. Is this not true knowledge of me?" says Yahweh in Jeremiah 22:16. This is the way older people and everyone else will be able to "know" God better and, through this knowledge, become more united with God in love.

A spirituality of older age in our times requires that each and every older person strive to understand the cultures of the world in which he or she lives. A better understanding of your present time will help you grow spiritually and discover the multiple facets of human beings, nature, art, and yourself. By integrating your faith in new ways in order to create a better world, you will be a signal — a lighthouse for the younger generation. Nothing can be more devastating for both you and future generations than attempting to practice spirituality without communicating with the culture that surrounds you. It is impossible to have a healthy spirituality if you isolate yourself from others.

There is not just *one* kind of spirituality of older age,

but many different kinds based on the uniqueness of each older person. Your religious opinions, your dialogue with others and with the natural world, and your personal insights into events of our time and culture form your own individual spiritual style. Such a mosaic can create the beauty and the strength of your spirituality and give meaning to your life.

SOURCES

[1]*Webster's New Collegiate Dictionary,* (Springfield, MA: Merriam-Webster, Inc. 1977).

[2]Arden Barden, "Toward New Directions for Ministry in Aging: An Overview of Issues and Concepts," *Journal of Religion and Aging,* Vol. 2½ (1985), p. 144.

[3]Viktor Frankl, *Man's Search for Meaning* (Boston: Beacon Press, 1985).

[4]Leo E. Missinne and Judy Welleke-Kay, "Reflections on the Meaning of Life in Older Age," *Journal of Religion and Aging,* Vol. 1, No. 4 (1985), p. 47.

[5]Viktor Frankl, *The Doctor of the Soul* (New York: Bantam Books, 1965), pp. IX-X.

[6]Joseph G. Donders, *Non-Bourgeois Theology* (New York: Orbis Books, 1985), p. 99.

[7]W. Paul Jones, "Gerontheology: Spirituality and Aging," *Quarterly Papers on Religion and Aging* Vol. 1, No. 1, (1984), p. 2.

[8]Henri Nouwen, *Reaching Out: The Three Movements of Spiritual Life* (Garden City, NY: Doubleday, 1986), p. 34.

[9]John S. Mbiti, *African Religions and Philosophy* (Garden City, NY: Anchor Books, 1969), p. 2.

[10]Helder Camara, *Hoping Against All Hope* (New York: Orbis Books, 1984).

[11]Howard Y. McClusky, "Educational for Aging: The Scope of the Field and Perspectives for the Future" in Stanley Grabowski and W. Dean Mason (eds.) *Learning for Aging* (Washington, DC: Adult Education Association of the USA, 1976), pp. 354-355.

[12]Robert C. Peck, "Psychological Development in the Second Half of Life" in Bernice Neugarten (ed.) *Middle Age and Aging* (Chicago: University of Chicago Press, 1968), p. 91.

CHAPTER FOUR

Toward a Theology of Living, Aging, and Dying

If I can stop one Heart from breaking
I shall not live in vain....

Emily Dickinson

What is life? What is aging? What is death?

These basic and difficult questions become still more complex and delicate when you have to reflect on your *own* life, your *own* older age, and your *own* death. To approach the challenges of life, older age, and death in a theological perspective is a challenge because most of us are not theologians; we are just average older persons trying our best to be good human beings.

When one utters the word *theology*, one has to first define it before linking it to life and death. Theology is the systematized knowledge of God's nature and the relations of God with human beings and the universe. Theology deals with God as related to human life when its studies deal with the origin and the essence of human life in its stages of development — childhood, adolescence, adulthood, and older age.

What are the relations of God toward persons in later life, and what are the relations of older persons toward God in their living and dying process? To answer these questions, let's first reflect on the theology of living in general.

A Theology of Living

In order to better understand the essence of what a Christian theology of living could mean, it's important to contrast it with two important aspects of life in the Western world, especially in the United States. The first is the drive toward power, and the second is the obsession with techniques. It is impossible to understand the behavior of human beings in Western culture if we do not take into account these two aspects.

Since the beginnings of our culture, people's desires for power have been the origin of inventions, behavior, and progress. The "number one" mentality of the United States has been and still is the basis of many American people's thoughts and actions. Americans tend to feel disappointed if they are only "number two." They want to be the best employee, the best teacher, or the best custodian of the year, the month, and even of the week! Competition, which is the motor that drives that power instinct, has given Western culture many advantages during all these years. We dominate the world economically and militarily, but in the meantime we have oppressed people from Third World countries and used their resources for our own benefits.

On an individual basis, this drive for power is often translated into a drive for money. The almighty dollar becomes the symbol of power — the symbol of a better and happier life. People with money are admired and offered as ideals for younger generations, giving the message that it is good to become rich as fast as possible and as young as possible.

A second aspect of Western culture is the importance of *techniques*. It often seems that everything we are and everything we do can be reduced to a question of knowing and applying the right techniques. We live in a very complicated technical world of computers and numbers. We often try to solve our economic, social, and human problems by using computers. A person who is not involved in this technical world and who does not understand it feels lost in our culture. Gibson Winter wrote in his book *Liberating Creation: Foundations of Religious Social Ethics*[1] that we are convinced that we can solve all our problems and make our world better through more and more technical inventions.

Christianity has been contaminated by these two aspects of Western culture. Our theology has become a theology of power and techniques, too. The Church has tried to become a power Church — an institution with political, economic, and financial power. God has become a power figure in our theology. He is almighty and the Master of the whole world. He dominates the world and is King of the kings. The Church has also tried to become a more technical and less personal institution. People too often see membership in a parish as a matter of applying certain techniques — doing mechanically what the priest says, registering in the parish, and contributing financially to the parish community.

Authentic Christianity is *not* based on power and techniques. Living as a Christian means to live as a human being, related to God, in harmony with God, and in harmony with other people and nature.

God, through the revelation of Christ, is love and not power. Proclaiming that God is love signifies clearly that God does not dominate the world. Love can even be seen as the opposite of domination. Love means respecting the other in his or her authenticity and helping the other in self-realization. God is love. That means that God respects the freedom of each human being and helps that human being grow toward a rich life of integrity.

God is helping human beings become better...not through dominating them or through divine techniques, but through invitations. God is an *inviting* God. That seems to be the most fundamental aspect of the image of our God who invites us to do good things. God invites us in the direction of goodness, harmony, beauty, and truth. Once in a while we see glimpses of this inviting

God when we encounter a good human being, when we try to make the world better by loving and sharing, when we enjoy music or a beautiful work of art. These glimpses of the inviting God are also realized in people such as Mother Teresa or Saint Francis, and others who have lived Christ's doctrine and made it their own way of life. They have transcended their lives by becoming inspiring invitations for others. They have become for us, images of the true, inviting God.

A Theology of Dying

There seem to be three typical aspects of death in our society.

Death is seen as an evil end to life. Death is seen as an evil because it's the end of a struggle for a particular individual. We don't like to talk about death in our culture because we feel that we have been defeated, that all of our techniques and power could not keep a person alive. We feel our powerlessness in the presence of death. It is the end of a fight which has been lost by the dead person and the doctors, and we don't like to lose.

Death is a taboo subject. Death is a prohibited topic in our society. We don't talk about it unless it's really necessary. We will use euphemisms such as "she passed away" or "he is no longer with us" in order keep ourselves from uttering the word *dead*. We will never be as beautiful in life as the day that we are lying in our casket.

People who never complimented us when we were alive will talk about how beautiful we are after we are dead. People will never give us so many flowers in such beautiful arrangements as on the day we are buried. People will never say so many nice things about us than they will after we cannot hear them. In fact, the whole funeral service is not for the dead person but for the survivors. It gives them the opportunity to see one another, to talk about themselves, and even about what will happen to the belongings of the "dearly departed"!

Death is a big business. It is expensive to die in the Western world. It has become a great ceremonial event with the dead person at the center of the proceedings. Fighting death by taking out life insurance is a contradictory act. Life insurance (which is actually death insurance) only insures a better financial life for the survivors.

Against this picture of death in Western society, what can death mean for a Christian? We must understand death in relation to the gift of life. Only people who have lived will die. God created us so that we could live and live abundantly. God created us so that we could enjoy the beauty of one anothers' existence. God could have created somebody else, but instead created you. If you are grateful for God's giving you the gift of life, in spite of all the difficult moments, at the time of your death you will be able to have everlasting life. The whole experience of your dying process will enhance your individuality and your gratitude to God who gives you life every day, month, and year to *live*.

No one can die in your place. Nothing is so personal as to die, even though dying is the most common human experience. At that time, what is most universal will become your own intimate experience of knowing that you are dying. Death will make of you that "particular individual" who will begin a personal life in and with God. Death will be the seal that you really are an individual ready for eternal life. In fact, for a Christian, death can be the greatest of all human blessings.

We must also understand death in relation to faith, hope, and love. The fact that you will someday die asks that you have faith in God's promises of eternal life — a faith already started in your innermost heart here on earth. Faith will help you see your death as a beginning and your life on earth as a preparation. Death creates hope in the heart of a Christian — hope for surviving an earthly life by knowing that a future life of happiness will be the reward. For Christians, death should create an incentive to love God and neighbor more so that we are better prepared for an intense love relationship with God after our earthly life. Dying means entering that moment in which we are totally alone with God and when the final decision about our life has to be made. At that moment we will see our weakness but also God's greatness and grace. At the hour of death, *all* becomes faith, hope, and love — faith in a God who knows and loves us in spite of our wrongdoings; hope in God's mercy; and, above all, trust and confidence in God's love.

A Theology of Living and Dying in Older Age

Where we came from and where we are going are mysteries. Life and death are mysteries. No one understands this better than older people. They know what life is all about because they have experienced it fully. They have known sufferings and joys, and the joys may cause them to sense that death could be the beginning of an eternal joy — a life of love and happiness.

"All joy wants eternity," said the German philosopher Friedrich Nietzsche. We older people can detect the most important values of life because we have experienced life in all its forms. God also shows us older people some of the mysteries about life and death before receiving us. The physical limitations of older age can refine our vision, helping us to look for the genuine values and beauty which will survive life on earth.

The Church can play a special role in helping us live out these revealed mysteries and real values in order to make our later years some of the most meaningful ones. Just as there is a sacrament for the beginning of life and for all the important phases of life, it would be good to have something of a new sacrament at the beginning of older age. This would be a special ceremony in which older people could consecrate themselves to some important tasks that could include things like committing to the great causes of justice; preserving a clean environment; developing a deeper bond of love and service for fellow human beings; and preparing themselves for the final encounter with their Creator.

One of the essential components of Judaism, which is called *mitzvah*, should be an inspiring example for older Christian people. The Jewish concept of mitzvah — religious obligation — provides older Jews with guides for living with a sense of dignity and meaning. Through mitzvah (mitzvoth is the plural) a person fulfills his or her obligations of the covenant between God and humanity. Mitzvoth are concrete acts that encompass all of life. Some examples of mitzvoth are the Jewish laws regarding eating, studying, divorce, business practice, prayer, procreation, care of the sick, care of the elderly, burial, and mourning. There are 613 of these charitable acts which turn everyday life into the sacred. Mitzvoth let the divine emerge from people's simple human deeds. The concept of mitzvah gives individual Jews of all ages and states of health the opportunity to experience a profound sense of self-worth and social value.

Abraham Heschel contends that it is in the experience of being obligated that one freely exists. That is also true for older people.

What a person lives by is not only a sense of belonging but a sense of indebtedness. The need to be needed corresponds to a fact, something is asked of a man, of every man. Advancing in years must not be taken to mean a process of suspending the requirements and commitments under which a person lives. To be is to obey.[2]

When a person begins performing mitzvoth out of the pure desire to do good and not only out of a sense of duty, he or she is on the way to becoming a wise person. The same is true for Christian people. If we are sick or handicapped older people, we are still obligated to do something for the community. We, too, are members of the Christian community to which we belong through Baptism. Christians believe that they should help and pray for sick older people. That is good, but the corresponding aspect has been forgotten: The elderly members of a community deserve to have an obligation too. We are obligated to try to be examples of Christian forgiveness, Christian faith, and Christian love. We older people must realize our continuing obligation to be active Christians. We must help one another find meaning in life and meaning in our suffering.

Older age could be an invitation that God is extending to you — a grace that allows you to move from the "many things" to one "necessary thing." It is true that God comes to people in different ways during their lives, but

God comes in a special way in your older age if you are in harmony with your aging, if you start to detach from your own possessions, if you free yourself from professional and social competition, and if you have the courage to surrender yourself to God. If you have been living just for physical appearance, older age will be a decay; but if you have been living in the Spirit, older age could be the ultimate encounter with the Spirit who is God. Living and dying well are only possible if you have come to grips with the difficult realities of your own life and your own death. If you are to live and die as a Christian, you must have a deep faith in God and a genuine love for God and your fellow human beings. Likewise, you will never be able to help another person in his or her dying process if you, yourself, are not alive — if you do not consciously enjoy life as a gift from God. Being conscious of your own finitude — your death — will help you live more intensely and more closely to God. Death can help you be grateful for each day or each hour you receive from God. The intensity of your life can help you have a better death. The fullness of life, which is the fullness of love, will help you go to God, the source of love which we will encounter after death.

In facing your own death, you can find great creativity, which has its roots in our capacity to love. In Henrik Ibsen's play *When We Dead Awake*, a woman tells us about a painter who had a model for his paintings. She loved him very much, but he did not permit himself to love her. One day he asked her, "When we dead awaken, what shall we find?" and she said, "We shall find that we have never lived."[3]

Some people will never die because they have never *lived* in the first place. You can only *live* if you *love*. The theology of living, aging, and dying is in fact the theology of respect for the *mystery* of life and death. Nobody dies from the darkness, but from the cold.

SOURCES

[1]Gibson Winter, *Liberating Creation: Foundations of Religious Social Ethics* (New York: Crossroads, 1981).

[2]Abraham J. Heschel, "To Grow in Wisdom," *The Insecurity of Freedom: Essays on Human Existence* (New York: Schocken, 1985), p. 78.

[3]Henrik Ibsen, "When We Dead Awake," *Ghosts and Other Plays* (New York: Penguin, 1964).

CONCLUSION

The Blessings of Older Age

Whether you are a member of the clergy, a religious, or a layperson, nothing is as good to know in older age as the Beatitudes. They are, literally, "be attitudes" — attitudes for being. Though the Beatitudes are an inspiration, they are not easy to practice. They are the comprehensive descriptions of Christian life.

Blessed are the poor in spirit,
for theirs is the kingdom of heaven.
Blessed are they who mourn,
for they will be comforted.
Blessed are the meek,
for they will inherit the land.
Blessed are they who hunger and thirst for righteousness,
for they will be satisfied.
Blessed are the merciful,
for they will be shown mercy.
Blessed are the clean of heart,
for they will see God.

Blessed are the peacemakers,
    for they will be called children of God.
Blessed are they who are persecuted for the sake
    of righteousness,
    for theirs is the kingdom of heaven.
Blessed are you when they insult you and per-
secute you and utter every kind of evil against you
[falsely] because of me. Rejoice and be glad, for
your reward will be great in heaven. Thus they
persecuted the prophets who were before you.

                    (Matthew 5:3-12)

It is so good to know that we are and will be blessed
by God in the many difficult events in our lives. The
Beatitudes express the spirit of genuine Christian life,
and genuine Christian life is a blessing. These words
offer an ideal that every Christian man or woman is
invited to realize. No people are closer to that Christian
ideal of the Beatitudes than we older adults because we
have experienced so much that has become a blessing
for us and for the people we meet.

Blessed are the people who are not attached to
earthly possessions. No one knows better than an older
person that earthly possessions do not give happiness
or peace and that they must be left behind at the end
of life.

Blessed are the people who are grieving, because

Christ has said that he is very close to those who are mourning the death of a spouse, a child, a grandchild, or a friend.

Blessed are the people who show mercy to those who have hurt them. Mercy and forgiveness that you have shown during your life will have their blessings in older age; they will give you a deep sense of peace.

Blessed are the people who have faith like a little child's, because that is the only way to see God. Deep faith and confidence in God are characteristics of so many older people. For that they will be blessed.

Blessed are the peacemakers, because they are doing the work of God. So many seniors have been peace-makers in the family problems of their children, grand-children, and friends. Because of their accumulated experience, they have become accepted arbitrators who have initiated a new atmosphere of understanding.

Blessed are the people who are not accepted and not respected in their Christian way of life. These people will have their reward in heaven!

Reflecting on all these blessings can make you happy in your later years. This happiness must not be kept, but shared. In sharing your hard-won happiness with younger generations, you can exemplify what positive aging can be. Nothing can influence younger people more than the grace of older adults at peace with God, themselves, and others.

By being living examples of love, happiness, goodness, forgiveness, patience, and generosity, as Christ told us to be, you can work miracles in the world today. The world needs examples of Christian love and goodness given in a practical way by experienced people. Look at the profound influence of Mother Teresa, Dr. Albert Schweitzer, or Padre Pio.

Try not to get caught up in examining only yourself; look around, and help your fellow human beings in becoming better Christians. Seniors can help one another to be peacemakers, to be merciful, to be happy, to forgive, to have more faith, more hope, and more love. That must be the purpose of the years that God gives you on this earth. If we all open our eyes and our ears, we will discover very quickly that many people are in need. In helping the needy, in helping one another, we will be closer to God and know God better, because God manifests himself many times in the needs of our fellow human beings.

If and when the day comes that you are no longer active, look to the example of Simeon and Anna in the story of Jesus' Presentation in the Temple. Simeon was a just and pious man waiting to see the Messiah. Anna was a widow constantly in the temple worshiping. She talked about the Messiah to all she encountered. The Holy Spirit revealed to Simeon and Anna that they would not experience death until they had seen Jesus, the Messiah. They set a fine example as older persons waiting for Jesus' coming into their our own hearts and into the hearts of humanity. Maybe you, too, could ask God that you not experience death until you have seen Jesus closely in your own thoughts and in the faces of the people you serve. Your prayer at the end of your life could be the same as that of Simeon: "Now Master, you may let your servant go in peace, according to your word, for my eyes have seen your salvation..." (Luke 2:29-30).

The perfect manner in which to age gracefully for a Christian is to balance a growing spirit against a declining body. Years will hack away some of the physical aspects of your body, but everything that is taken away from you will uncover your spirit — your inner being, that is becoming more like Christ. Older age will show us all what we really are. Maybe you will be surprised by the beauty of your spirit and the strength of your faith, your hope, and your love for God.

Some people agree that in their older age they are becoming increasingly aware of a surprising thing emerging within them — something that people have become accustomed to calling "spirit." This spirit is often in better condition than when their physical bodies were at their best. This phenomenon casts doubt on the theory that says people must have healthy bodies in order to have healthy minds. Saint Paul announced the same idea when he wrote: "Therefore, we are not discouraged; rather, although our outer self is wasting away, our inner self is being renewed day by day" (2 Corinthians 4:16).

This idea helps us envision the process that is going on in an aging person.

There was once a young woman who visited the studio of the great artist Michelangelo. She was grieved to see him hacking away at the beautiful marble and argued with the illustrious sculptor and painter about what he was wasting. She pointed to the growing pile of chips that littered the floor. But Michelangelo said, "The more the marble wastes, the more the statue grows."

The years hack away the beauty of our bodies, but each part that time takes away unveils an inner being who is becoming more like Christ — the source and essence of all Christian life. Each stage in our lives is the beginning of a new aspect of Christian life. Our older age can be the beginning of our closest encounter with God.

Older age is a time to give thanks:
For the joy of having been loved by God during such a long life.
For the ability to run through the souvenirs of so many graces received.
For the understanding that this is a time for trust, detachment, and serenity.

Older age is a time to pray:
For those whom I love and whom I shall soon leave.
For those who have no time to pray.

Older age is the specific time:

When I think about what is essential in life.

When I make time to forgive those who hurt me.

When I unite myself in contemplation and meditation with my God.

When I start to see things and others with my heart.

Bibliography

Bianchi, Eugene. *Aging as a Spiritual Journey.* New York: Crossroad, 1984.

Buber, Martin. *I and Thou.* New York: Scribner, 1970.

Buscaglia, Leo. *Personhood: The Art of Being Fully Human.* New York: Fawcett Columbine, 1988.

Cole, Thomas R., and Sally A. Gadow. *What Does It Mean to Grow Old: Reflections From the Humanities.* Durham, NC: Duke University Press, 1986.

Crumbaugh, James C. *Everything to Gain: A Guide to Self-Fulfillment Through Logoanalysis.* Chicago: Nelson-Hall, 1973.

Daniels, Victor, and Laurence Horowitz. *Being and Caring: A Journey to Self.* Palo Alto, CA: Mayfield, 1976.

DeBellis, Robert, et. al., eds. "Suffering, Psychological and Social Aspects in Loss, Grief, and Care." *Loss, Grief and Care: A Journal of Professional Practice,* Vol. 1, No. 1, 2, 1986-87.

Dougherty, Flavian (ed.). *The Meaning of Human Suffering.* New York: Human Science Press, 1982.

Erikson, Erik. *The Life Cycle Completed.* New York: Norton, 1982.

Fabry, Joseph B. *A Guide to the Theory and Application of Viktor E. Frankl's Logotherapy,* 1969. Cork and Dublin: Mercier Press, 1975.

_____*The Pursuit of Meaning: Logotherapy and Life.* Preface by Viktor E. Frankl. Boston: Beacon Press, 1968.

Farry, Joseph B., Reuven P. Bulka, and William S. Sahakian (eds.). *Logotherapy in Action.* New York: Jason Aronson, Inc., 1979.

Frankl, Viktor E. *Man's Search for Meaning: An Introduction to Logotherapy.* Boston: Beacon Press, 1985.

_____ *Psychotherapy and Existentialism: Selected Papers on Logotherapy.* New York: Touchstone, 1985.

_____ *The Will to Meaning: Foundations and Applications to Logotherapy.* New York: New American Library, 1988.

_____ *The Unconscious God: Psychotherapy and Theology.* New York: Simon and Schuster, 1985.

Fromm, Erich. *The Art of Loving.* New York: Perennial Library, Harper and Row, 1974.

_____ *Escape from Freedom.* New York: Avon, 1982.

Harris, Sydney. *The Authentic Person, Dealing with Dilemma.* Chicago: Argus Communications, 1972.

Hateley, B.J. *Telling Your Story, Exploring Your Faith.* St. Louis, Christian Board of Publication, 1985.

Howard, Alice and Walden. *Exploring the Road Less Traveled.* New York: Simon and Schuster, 1985.

Jourard, Sidney M. *The Transparent Self.* New York: Van Nostrand, 1971.

Jung, Carl G. *Modern Man in Search of a Soul.* New York: Harcourt Brace Jovanovich, 1955.

_____*Psychology and Western Religion: West and East.* Princteon, NJ: Princeton University Press, 1984.

Kaufman, Sharon R. *The Ageless Self: Sources of Meaning in Late Life.* Madison, WI: University of Wisconsin Press, 1986.

Kinget, G. Marian. *On Being Human, A Systematic View.* New York: Harcourt Brace Jovanovich, 1987.

Kushner, Harold. *When All You' ve Ever Wanted Isn't Enough.* New York: Summit Books, 1987.

Levinas, Emmanuel. *Totality and Infinity.* Pittsburgh: Duquesne University Press, 1969.

Maddi, Salvatore and Paul Costa. *Humanism in Personology.* Chicago: Adline-Atherton, 1972.

Maslow, Abraham. *Toward a Psychology of Being.* New York: Van Nostrand, 1968.

May, Rollo. *Existence.* New York: Basic Books, 1958.

_____ *Love and Will.* New York: W. W. Norton, 1969.

Missinne, Leo E. "Meaning of Life in Older Age." *Quarterly Papers on Religion and Aging,* Vol. 1, No. 5, 1985.

_____"Three Approaches to the Mystery of Suffering: Frankl, Gray, and Kushner." *Quarterly Papers on Religion and Aging,* Vol 1, No. 4, 1985, pp. 43-58.

Missinne, Leo E., and Judy Willeke Kay. "Reflections on the Meaning of Life in Older Age." *Journal of Religion and Aging*. Vol. 1, No. 4, 1985, pp. 43-58.

Moustakas, Clark. *Individuality and Encounter.* Cambridge, MA: Howard A. Doyle, 1968.

_____*The Self, Explorations in Personal Growth.* New York: Harper Torchbooks, Harper and Row, 1974.

Nouwen, Henri J. and Walter Gaffney. *Aging: The Fulfillment of Life.* Garden City, NY: Image Books, Doubleday, 1976.

Nouwen, Henri J. *Reaching Out: The Three Movements of Spiritual Life.* Garden City, NY: Doubleday, 1986.

Peck, M. Scott. *The Road Less Traveled.* New York: Simon and Schuster, 1980.

Powell, John. *Why Am I Afraid to Love?* Valencia, CA: Tabor Publisher, 1972.

Rogers, Carl. *Becoming Partners.* New York: Delacorte, 1972.

_____*On Becoming a Person.* Boston: Houghton Mifflin, 1972.

Takashima, Hiroshi. *Psychosomatic Medicine and Logotherapy.* Foreword by Viktor E. Frankl. Oceanside, NY: Dabor Science Publications, 1977.

Tillich, Paul. *The Courage to Be.* New Haven, CT: Yale University Press, 1952.

_____*My Search for Absolutes.* New York: Simon and Schuster, 1967.

Tournier, Paul. *Learn to Grow Old*. New York: Harper and Row, 1983.

_____*The Meaning of Persons*. New York: Harper and Row, Perennial Library, 1983.

Tweedie, Donald F. *Logotherapy and the Christian Faith: An Evaluation of Frankl's Existential Approach to Psychotherapy.* Grand Rapids, MI: Baker Book House, 1972.

Ungersma, Aaron J. *The Search for Meaning: A New Approach to Psychotherapy and Pastoral Psychology.* Philadelphia: Westminster Press, 1968.

Weininger, Ben, and Eva L. Menkin. *Aging Is a Lifelong Affair.* Los Angeles: The Guild of Tutors Press, 1978.

Yalom, Irvin D. *Existential Psychotherapy.* New York: Basic Books, Inc., 1980.

ABOUT THE AUTHOR:

Father Leo E. Missinne is a professor of gerontology at the University of Nebraska, Omaha. He is also a visiting professor of gerontology at the University of Southern California. He is associated with the Center for the Study of Preretirement and Aging at the Catholic University of America, Washington, DC. He was ordained a Roman Catholic priest in 1953. He holds a Ph.D. in Educational Sciences from the University of Louvain in Belgium.